Overcoming Cor

Body Language
What You Need to Know

COHEN

sheldon**PRESS**

In memory of Dr James MacKeith,
good friend and wise shrink

First published in Great Britain in 2007

Sheldon Press
36 Causton Street
London SW1P 4ST

Copyright © David Cohen 2007

The author and publisher have made every effort to ensure that the
external website and email addresses included in this book are correct and
up to date at the time of going to press. The author and publisher are not
responsible for the content, quality or continuing accessibility of the sites.

British Library Cataloguing-in-Publication Data
A catalogue record for this book is available from the British Library

ISBN 978-1-84709-003-4

1 3 5 7 9 10 8 6 4 2

Typeset by Fakenham Photosetting Ltd, Fakenham, Norfolk
Printed in Great Britain by Ashford Colour Press

Produced on paper from sustainable forests

Contents

Illustrations

About the author

David Cohen is a psychologist and film-maker who has been study-ing body language off and on for the last 15 years. He is a Fellow of the Royal Society of Medicine and the author of both serious and not-so-serious books, including *Psychologists on Psychology* (interviews with some of the world's greatest psychologists), *Diana: Death of a Goddess, Mrs Beeton's Best Bits* (on the cookery diva) and *The Father's Book: Being a Good Dad in the 21st Century*. His film on Soham, *Our Daughter Holly*, was nominated for the BAFTA award for the best current affairs programme in 2005. His latest film, *Pushing the Limits*, is about Mark Eccleston, who captained Britain's wheel-chair rugby team. In real life David likes watching people's body language on the tube.

Introduction

We speak with our mouths, but we communicate with our eyes, our faces, our smiles, our hands, our arms, even with our legs and toes. Possibly the only part of our bodies we don't communicate with is our belly button – and I'm not sure that statement is true. After all, if you decorate your belly button with a metal stud, it reveals something of your personality: Stud Girl is not likely to be a shy wallflower.

No one can know whether dinosaurs used some form of scaly non-verbal communication or body language, but body language is almost certainly very ancient. There are studies of non-verbal communication in dogs, cats, horses and, even, cows. Chimps and gorillas use complex systems of non-verbal communication – and we have a lot in common with them. A famous book published in the 1960s, Desmond Morris's *The Naked Ape*, argued that a great deal of our behaviour is very similar to that of the apes.

Today body language is as important as it has ever been – perhaps even more so now that we live in a 24/7 fast-changing world, the stressed society. We meet new people all the time and have to make up our minds about them very quickly. Do we like them? Can they be trusted? Are they likely to attack us or will they be happy if we suggest going out on a date?

A hundred years ago people needed introductions in order to be let into someone's drawing room. Today, there are virtually no such formalities. If you have five minutes to decide whether the person sitting opposite might be a good colleague, the love of your life or a total loser, you need to understand their non-verbal communication. And that is not simple – for a simple reason.

Homo sapiens is the only species that can lie, deceive and try to imagine what someone has in mind. The most advanced ape can't imagine what another ape is thinking, or whether Chimp A hates his guts because he envies his chest hair. In terms of guile, spite, deception and self-knowledge, the chimp is a chump compared to us.

We, proud rulers of planet Earth, can perform marvels of duplicity. So we need help to work out what someone else is really thinking but that they may be too polite, confused, clever or manipulative to say.

As we shall see, individuals differ in how well they understand body language. People who suffer from autism and schizophrenia find body language almost impossible to grasp. According to psychologist Sergio Paradiso (1999) of the University of Iowa,

> as we interact with people, we make judgments that we're not consciously aware of. If we see a co-worker hunched over and don't see his face, we may approach him cautiously because we think something might be wrong and perhaps we can help. We don't see the face, but we glean information from the body language. People with schizophrenia are not as good at extracting this kind of information to guide their social interactions.

The consequences can be serious. If you don't read body language, you may upset people you have to deal with and so become even more nervous and socially awkward.

But it is not a simple question of intelligence. You may be very smart academically and still fail to read the signals other people give out. You may not shine at IQ tests but be perfectly able to sense what other people feel because you respond 'instinctively' to their body language.

Responding instinctively or with intuition is not a kind of magic. What we're really doing is collating, almost instantly, dozens of tiny clues we've picked up from a person's body language – the way they stand and hold themselves, the angles of their arms, the expression on their faces, where they are looking, even whether the pupils of their eyes are dilated or not.

Body language does not just tell us about others, however; it can reveal how we feel and worry – to ourselves. In the stressed-self society, we are apt to fret and feel neurotic. Stress makes us drink too much, use too many drugs, suffer psychosomatic ills and be very aware of our dissatisfactions. One way in which we show stress is through our body language: our tics – and antics. I rub my eyes because I feel worried, I shift the way I'm sitting and clasp my knees – both actions that comfort me. I notice I am fidgeting and realize I am more nervous about my next meeting than I want to admit.

Unconscious speaks and leaks

Case history

As Tony sits opposite his boss and the head of personnel, it is hard to tell whether he is up for promotion or about to be hauled over the coals. He looks relaxed. His boss is smiling, but there is a devious reason for that. There's a mirror behind Tony that allows his boss to see what Tony is trying to hide. Tony doesn't realize the mirror is there and thinks he is managing to hide his anxiety. But his hands are behind his back and he keeps twisting his fingers – a classic sign of nervous body language. Tony also rubs his cheek.

Good, thinks his boss. He wants to sack Tony and has hacked into his e-mails. Foolishly Tony has been involved in an e-mail exchange about buying cannabis. The company does not allow use of its e-mail for personal communication, let alone buying illegal drugs.

But the boss has no right to hack into other people's e-mails and he's been worried Tony might sue the company. Observing Tony's body language in the mirror, he can see Tony is scared and anxious to defend himself.

Over the next 15 minutes, the boss is vicious and he enjoys seeing the impact this has. Finally Tony closes his eyes, trying to shut this whole nightmare out. The boss wins; Tony lets himself be sacked without much fuss.

If his boss had not seen, and been able to understand, Tony's nervous body language, he would not have had the confidence to be so aggressive. But Tony couldn't control his body language and he paid the price.

Celebrity

Much body language is unconscious – and the twitch of an eyebrow, the tilt of a head, the turn of an arm can and often does say volumes more than the spoken word. Such movements are at the heart of our communication, as strangers, work colleagues, friends and lovers. So it's wise to try to understand body language better. By reading others more accurately, and by being more in control of what we project, our work, social and love life can only be enriched.

Body language also has a high profile today because of our obsession with celebrity. Women's magazines carry endless stories on the latest celebrity's body language. One FBI agent has even analysed Madonna's eyelid flutters to see if she was lying on NBC television when she denied she was pregnant.

For many years, of course, Madonna was not just a successful singer but an icon. She had the perfect body.

The perfect body

The media are full of images of perfect women and men, which creates anxiety and unrealistically high self-expectations in the rest of us. One-third of men and 70 per cent of women think they are too fat or too large. Body-image disorders are rife, including anorexia, bulimia and body dysmorphia (a disorder in which a person has a distorted view of his or her body or of a part of the body).

Yet our idea of the perfect body has changed. In 1917, for example, the physically perfect woman was about 1.6m (5ft 4in) tall and weighed 63kg (nearly 10 stone). In the early 1940s, people with thin, bony bodies were perceived as nervous, submissive and socially withdrawn. Marilyn Monroe, on the other hand, had the ideal female body – curvy or hourglass-shaped.

By the 1980s, however, curves were so yesteryear. Supermodels were rake-thin and an ounce of fat was – and is – a Greek tragedy. Even 25 years ago, however, top models and beauty queens weighed 8 per cent less than the average woman; now they weigh 23 per cent less. Only 5 per cent of women achieve what the media currently decree is the ideal weight and size.

It would help, in theory, if we had a more objective idea of how we look. If the old-fashioned mirror isn't good enough, it is possible to try 3D-imaging of the body. This is called body metrics. Some very new research by Professor Philip Treleaven of University College, London (2006) claims we can now know better than ever before what we look like and what we find attractive about other people. Since 1920, the average woman's breast size has increased by four inches, her hips by six inches, and her waist by eight inches, according to Treleaven. Despite all these changes in fashion, Treleaven's research suggests that, often, we still read bodies in age-old ways. For example, men tend to find the fuller female more attractive, while women prefer men with a very low percentage of body fat, whether they are thin or muscular. There are biological reasons for these preferences. Larger women may appear more fertile, or find it easier to give birth; a man with a big chest looks as if he can protect his family.

What is seen as the perfect body may change, but many aspects of body language do not. Body language – and how it is perceived – is embedded deep in our biological heritage, so that we are often not even aware of using the clues it provides. In this book I hope to offer a useful introduction to the latest research on body language – and practical tips that will help us to understand other people's body language and manage our own. The more we know about the art and science of body language, the better we will be at these very necessary skills.

Among the themes I cover are:

• meeting someone for the first time;
• dating;
• trying to work out how someone feels about you;
• trying to ascertain whether something is going wrong with your significant other.

And work situations such as:

• being interviewed for a job;
• being interviewed for a promotion;
• everyday dealings with colleagues, which can involve conflicts that sometimes get very tense.

Chapter 1 looks at the history of body language research and its controversies. Chapter 2 examines the basics of body language, and Chapter 3 considers how we make first impressions. Chapter 4 analyses the question of personal space, what it means and the conscious and unconscious moves we make to protect it. Chapter 5 looks at many small and not-so-small details of body language, such as what we do with our hands. Chapter 6 covers the latest research on eye contact. Chapter 7 summarizes 40 years of research into facial expressions: what we can read from people's faces and how we control our own facial expressions.

Chapter 8 moves into the work environment and examines body language in the office and the shop. It looks at body language in interviews, how to dissect the boss's tics and fidgets, and how to cope if you are in trouble at work. It also explains an unusual technique called 'paradoxical intention'. Chapter 9 looks at flirting, fancying and sex – how to tell if someone of the opposite sex is interested in you, and, just as important, how to tell if they're not. Chapter 10 examines lying: how to tell if people are lying to you and, yes, how to prevent your own body language reveal you are lying. Chapter 11 looks at body language in different cultures – and suggests why Arabs may find it hard to grasp the nuances of Japanese body language. Chapter 12 sums up what I hope readers will have learned.

1

The science of body language

The last few years have seen more 'serious' analysis of body language than ever before. Psychologists like Peter Collett and Geoffrey Beattie of Sheffield University – the psychologist on *Big Brother* – have new theories. The latest brain-imaging techniques allow scientists to see what parts of the brain work hard when people perform various tasks. Such imaging also makes it possible to see how body language depends on certain parts of the brain and what happens when those are damaged. Child psychologists have tracked how children develop body language skills – and what to do if they aren't developing them 'normally'.

Heaven sent

A good place to start is in 1853 in the small town of Lourdes in southwest France. A peasant girl, Marie Bernarde Soubirous (who came to be known as Bernadette), claimed she saw an apparition of the Virgin Mary in a grotto. Her neighbours were sceptical at first; Bernadette's family was poor and had been in trouble with the police. But people were soon persuaded that Bernadette had true visions because of the convincing way she gestured to her apparition.

Within two years, Lourdes was a famous shrine. Even the Church, which was always very worried that such visions were inspired by the Devil, accepted that the peasant girl had seen the Blessed Virgin. Today every year thousands of pilgrims visit Lourdes, possibly because Bernadette's body language was compelling and so inspired belief.

The rest of the book deals with thoroughly unspiritual matters like sex, power and office politics. But don't forget the religious connection. It's no accident that people often pray on their knees, one of the most submissive of all human positions. Muslims go even further than people of some other faiths and prostrate themselves before Allah.

Body language and lying

Exercise 1.1: Telling a lie

Imagine you are in a situation where you suspect someone of lying. Write down the five key things you look for in both their words and their body language.

As this is early in the book, you may need a few clues to gestures that often accompany lying – fidgeting with your fingers, touching your nose, fiddling with your hair ends, looking down and to the side, saying the lie while fiddling with a handbag, gloves or cigarettes. Some people argue that men and women who are very nervous may behave just like someone who is lying – and there is a germ of truth in that.

Total attention, total attraction

Carl Rogers (1902–1986), a famous American therapist, built a school of therapy on giving clients what he called 'unconditional personal regard'. It meant simply that when he sat across the desk

Figure 1.1 Unconditional personal regard

and listened to them, he let them know he was listening with total concentration (see Figure 1.1). Some of his techniques were:

- He gave clients time to talk.
- He nodded his head to encourage them to go on.
- He waited patiently when they paused.
- He often leaned forward to create a more intimate feeling of rapport.

Many of us are not born listeners but there is nothing that mysterious about developing the skill, just as there is nothing mysterious in understanding most aspects of your own personality – something you need to know if you are to become an MBL: a *Maestro of Body Language*.

Exercise 1.2: Know-yourself test

Use a scale of 1–5, where

5 means always true of me
4 means quite often true of me
3 means sometimes true of me
2 means very occasionally true of me
1 means never true of me.

How do you rate yourself on the following questions:

1 I worry about what people think of me.
2 I ask myself why I behave the way I do.
3 I check myself in the mirror before I go out.
4 I get nervous when someone I think of as a friend acts in a way I don't understand.
5 I worry that I am far too vain.
6 I get nervous when I go into a room and I know no one there.
7 I like to try to work out what other people are thinking.
8 There are certain things about other people's body language I always notice.
9 I think it is important to be calm, cool and collected.
10 I wish I looked different – was better looking, like Nicole Kidman or Brad Pitt – but I don't lose sleep over it.
11 I find it hard to concentrate on listening to what other people have to say.

12 I am often anxious that I may not make a good impression.
13 I like observing other people.
14 I like observing other people when they don't realize I'm doing it.
15 It bothers me that other people may guess what I'm thinking by just looking at me.

Answers
In theory you could score 75 on this test.

Questions 1–6, 12 and 15 assess your anxieties about the impression you make. If you are always anxious about these issues, you could score as high as 40 on these questions. The utterly unanxious will score 8.

- A total of 30–40 suggests you are very anxious about how you present your body language.
- A score of 20–30 suggests you are somewhat anxious about this.
- Under 20 suggests you are quite relaxed about this.

Questions 7–11, 13 and 14 are about detachment and being curious about body language. You could score 35 on these questions.

- If you score between 25 and 35 you are very curious about other people's body language and quite detached.
- If you score 15 to 25 you are averagely curious and averagely detached.
- If you score under 15 you really aren't interested in other people's body language – and are missing fascinating clues about how people behave.

Controversy

Today, experts on body language are in the middle of a controversy. Traditionalists claim you can divorce non-verbal behaviour almost entirely from words. Perhaps the most extreme claims are made by a Californian psychologist, Professor Albert Mehrabian. He said in the 1970s that:

- 7 per cent of meaning is in the words that are spoken;
- 38 per cent of meaning is paralinguistic (the way that the words are said);
- 55 per cent of meaning is in the facial expression that accompanies the words.

Non-verbal cues account for 93 per cent of the meaning we take from any interaction, according to Mehrabian (1972). Many people accept these statistics. In theory, therefore, if I smile sweetly and sound like a cooing dove while I tell you that you are an unpleasant person, you'll not pay that much attention to the 'unpleasant' part of the message and won't be upset. After all, 93 per cent of my message (the smile and the cooing) is positive.

I wouldn't try that approach myself. Most people do seem to mind if you call them unpleasant. So it is no surprise Mehrabian's ideas are contradicted in the works of artists and scientists – including those of William Shakespeare among others. The idea that your gestures matter more than your words flies in the face of the advice Hamlet delivers to the Player King, the leader of the troupe of actors who came to the court of the King of Denmark:

> Suit the action to the word, the word to the action with this special observance – that you o'erstep not the modesty of nature.

That's still good advice for actors.

Many scientists, including *Big Brother* psychologist Geoffrey Beattie in his *Visible Language* (2004), think that psychology should catch up with Hamlet. Words and gestures go together and should be considered jointly as a communication package, not split into different bits as Mehrabian suggests. And the result is that body language is even more revealing, Beattie claims: 'We now recognise that much of our body language is fleeting and, rather than revealing emotions, it actually reveals what we are thinking as well.'

Darwin had a word for it

Philosophers in ancient Greece argued 'that the good and evil passions by their continual exercise stamp their impress on the face, and that each particular passion has its own expression'. The Greek poet Homer observed how expression and appearance 'correlated with character'.

Some 2,000 years later, in 1600, Sir Francis Bacon, the Lord Chancellor of England, said you could learn 'the disposition of the mind by the lineaments of the body'. This science came to be known as physiognomy, but it did not have a very good reputation as many of those who claimed to practise it were in it only for the money. There were so many abuses that an Act of Parliament in 1743 condemned 'all persons pretending to have skill in physiognomy as rogues and vagabonds' to be publicly whipped, or sent to jail.

Luckily that law doesn't seem to be practised now. Otherwise I – and many fellow authors of body language books – would be in the nick.

By 1872, it was safe for the eminently respectable Charles Darwin to publish *The Expression of the Emotions in Man and Animals*. Darwin, the father of the theory of evolution, had noticed that apes used certain gestures over and over again; he got scientists from all over the world to send him interesting examples of such 'animal language', as he called it. Darwin wanted to see if there were any links between human gestures and animal gestures. He got hundreds of replies, especially descriptions of teeth-baring, laughter and displays of triumph, when apes tended not just to thump their chests but also to leap, run and yelp.

I would never suggest that today's footballers remotely resemble gorillas, but shall we say that when certain ball wizards score they behave in ways Darwin would have recognized (see Figure 1.2).

Figure 1.2 Man and ape

The alpha ape thumps his chest after socking it to a lesser ape. The triumphant alpha-male footballer, when he has socked the ball into the net, runs frenetically, cartwheels and hugs his team mates. Most footballers don't thump their chests like King Kong, but there is no mistaking the meaning of their ritual dance. It trumpets 'I am the top dog, top ape, top foot, top banana.'

There are some differences between the ace gorilla and the ace sharp-shooter, however. For one, the gorilla is far too inhibited to get involved in a celebratory group hug. The group hug for sports teams has now even spread to cricket, once that most reserved of sports. W. G. Grace must be turning in his grave.

And the centre forward is unlikely to urinate either in the goal (which he has conquered) or over his opponents in sheer hot-shot exuberance.

The gorilla will not blow a kiss to the crowd.

The centre forward, if he has been getting a bad press, may race at the crowd wagging his finger manically. Gorillas do not go in for this gesture, perhaps because they don't care about bad write-ups in *The Daily Ape*.

Exercise 1.3: Self-observation

When was the last time you felt triumphant?

How did you behave?

Were you happy for other people to see just how energized you felt?

If you wanted to hide it, what did you do to conceal your sense of triumph?

Tip

Beware of showing how good you feel when you have triumphed. It is apt to make people resentful unless they really love you and approve of your success. Most people are more ambivalent.

Darwin even speculated that you can spot a selfish character just from non-verbal cues: 'Slyness is also, I believe, exhibited chiefly by movements about the eyes; for these are less under the control of the will, owing to the force of long-continued habit, than are the movements of the body' (1872: 484).

After Darwin there was little academic study of body language until the 1960s when two men turned their attention to the subject and made it both popular and academically respectable. One was the zoologist Desmond Morris, who wrote *The Naked Ape* (1967), showing how much human behaviour was similar to that of gorillas, baboons and chimps.

The second writer was a quirky man who taught me psychology when I was at Oxford. Michael Argyle was tall, rather awkward and not always subtle. He used to stick a pillow under his bottom which made him sit up far taller than us students. The taller you sat, the more superior you were, he told us as he patted the pillow. For a distinguished academic, he had some surprising insecurities. But his ideas on height were sound, as we shall see.

Argyle (1975) argued that most people when they look straight at you are being sincere. The eyes are the windows to the soul.

But not with everyone.

Some people have a *Machiavellian personality* type. Argyle gave it that name after the famous sixteenth-century Italian author, Niccolo Machiavelli. Machiavelli wrote the key text on how to be ruthless in politics, *The Prince*. Some modern politicos even admit they still consult it, as it has timeless tips for the vital arts of plotting, leaking information and stabbing colleagues in the back.

Machiavellian types, Argyle said, are so naturally devious that they can look someone straight in the eye, sound as sincere as a saint – and lie all the while.

Shakespeare understood Machiavellian types. He made his villain Richard III say:

Why I can smile
And murder whilst I smile
And cry content to that which gives me pause.

Shakespeare knew both that gestures normally reinforce what we say, as Hamlet said, and that they do not have to. Freud was right to think the Bard was the greatest instinctive psychologist who ever lived.

Machiavellians are so much in command of their body language that they can give out very controlled signals. They appear so convincing because these are precisely the kind of signals we assume to be unconscious and automatic. But Machiavellians use them to give the illusion that they are being sincere when they are really being highly manipulative. For instance, the Machiavellian stares straight at you while lying (Figure 1.3).

Figure 1.3 The Machiavellian

Are people born Machiavellian or do they learn to become like that?

Body language starts young

We start to learn body language at birth. We suck, cry, grasp with our hands and, within four to five weeks, smile. By six to nine months we point at things. Within two years of starting to speak, toddlers learn one human truth – you can say things you don't mean and not mean things you do say.

When they are about three years old, toddlers take their first steps in what has to be our lifelong study, the psychology of other people. No one tells toddlers to start being Freud in nappies so they can understand what other people's gestures mean, but unless they are affected by either an autistic disorder or Asperger's syndrome, they do it anyway. By the age of four, the normal toddler will have learned a good deal about what gestures mean; he or she will also know the difference between reality and pretending.

Just to make it easy for children to know the boundary between the real and the not-real, we often make exaggerated gestures or play faces when we start to pretend (Figure 1.4).

Figure 1.4   The play face

Four-year-olds also know that it is not smart to put your hand over your mouth when telling a fib. Under stress, however, even sophisticated adults can forget that. Watch our political leaders the next time they appear on TV to see if you can spot whether they are telling the truth – where are their hands?

The hand or the fingers hide the mouth because the mouth is 'ashamed' not to be telling the truth (Figure 1.5). It is much the same principle when, as a child, we mime 'shush'. Argyle (1975) also made much of the not very elegantly named concept of *leaks* which some psychologists, like Peter Collett (2005), now call *tells*.

The theory again owes something to Freud. In *The Psychopathology of Everyday Life* (1930), he gave many examples of 'parapraxes', as he called them, of people forgetting things or making peculiar mistakes. The unconscious is primitive and teems with taboo desires that tend to erupt. Freud described one woman patient who

Figure 1.5   A sign of lying: a hand over the mouth

insisted she was happy in her marriage but kept on fiddling with her wedding ring, taking it off and putting it back on her finger. You didn't have to be a genius to work out she was ambivalent about her husband. Unconscious motives and wishes will get out. Not all of them are as telling or transparent, however, as the wedding-ring fidget.

The *tell* started as a term in poker but is now becoming part of popular culture. In *Casino Royale*, the first Bond film to star Daniel Craig, there is much talk of tells when 007 plays poker against the evil Le Chiffre. Bond wins, but he is not that smart a reader of body language as he fails to spot that his new girlfriend is actually on the side of the baddies. She is a true Machiavellian.

Celebrity, politics and body language

During the period of rivalry between Gordon Brown and Tony Blair, their body language fascinated the media. In 2004, the *Daily Mail* asked Peter Collett, the author of the theory of tells, to study videotapes of the Chancellor and the Prime Minister, as they were then.

However hard the two men tried, their toes and fingers leaked the truth that they were bitter rivals. During Tony Blair's speech at the 2004 party conference, the Chancellor 'fidgeted a staggering 322 times. This included 15 separate soothing fiddles with his cuffs, and numerous glances at the floor, as well as folding his arms and stroking his face,' Collett counted.

'Mr. Blair also betrays his insecurity by stroking his stomach – a sign of seeking a mother's comfort,' Collett added. Mothers often rub a baby's tummy to comfort them. 'Tony's mother is not there to rub his tummy for him, so he does it himself,' explained the *Psycho Mail*.

In 2006 things got worse. Gordon Brown was praising Tony Blair when he leaked like a ship in a storm. He touched his nose.

Touching the nose, many experts argue, is a 'displacement activity' which suggests a person is lying. But the idea that touching the nose shows that someone is lying comes from a fairy tale. In the old story of Pinocchio, his nose grows every time he tells a lie. It has been suggested that a liar touches his nose because blood flow increases when lying. So what seems a nervous tic is, in fact, a devious tic. The nose toucher is trying to conceal his hooter, which has become engorged and grows redder as more blood flows into it.

Exercise 1.4: Self-observation

One day jot down every time you touch your nose – and what you were saying or thinking at the time. How often were you lying?

Popular interest in body language has had its consequences. When Desmond Morris and Michael Argyle started work in the 1960s, only psychologists had much sense of what it was. Today we are all very aware of it, in the developed world at least. We are no longer naïve about some of the most obvious signs of body language. That makes it both more complicated and more interesting to understand and to observe.

One key concept we need to grasp is that of the displacement activity.

Displacement activity

Psychologists define a displacement activity as 'the performance of an act inappropriate for the stimulus that evokes it'. When an ostrich is frightened because it sees a leopard is about to pounce, the intelligent thing would be to run. Instead the ostrich often buries its head in the sand, which does not scare off any predators but presumably de-stresses the distressed ostrich – at least for a few seconds.

Displacement activities usually occur when an animal is torn between two conflicting drives, such as wanting a mate and being frightened because another bird after the same mate is bigger and has sharper claws. Some birds facing such a dilemma perch on one leg.

Humans go in for displacement activities too, though they don't often bury their heads in the sand or perch on one leg. Common displacement activities are scratching behind the ear (Figure 1.6), putting the arms behind the back and pacing up and down. When small children are being told off by their parents they quite often put their hand behind their head and avoid their parents' eyes. Some people – and animals – also drink and eat. The man who is unsure how to handle his date may munch endless crisps and peanuts at the bar.

Figure 1.6   A displacement activity: scratching behind the ear

Body language provides clues to stress – and to even more serious conditions.

Body language and mental health

In the nineteenth century, psychiatrists often photographed their patients so that they could catch a perfect example of depression or hysteria. Some of these pictures are quite grotesque. If you go into a psychiatric hospital today, even one like Broadmoor which houses the criminally insane, you will not see the florid 'mad' body language that was typical 150 years ago. Drugs can now suppress many symptoms. But you will still see people hunched up on their beds, lying on the floor curled up in the foetal position or sitting slumped in an armchair. These are all classic signs of clinical depression. You will also see some patients who pace and pace and pace. This is partly anxiety, partly the side-effects of drugs.

One extreme form of destructive body language that is very distressing, as well as symbolic, is head-banging. Disturbed children often bang their heads against a wall, and so do disturbed adults. Some head-bangers say they are trying to expel the evil spirits – and that this is the only way they think they can do it.

Slowly, psychologists have realized the importance of body language in mental illness. One rather imaginative experiment reveals how profound the inability to understand body language can be.

Subjects watched a video of human bodies in motion. The bodies were expressing happiness or sadness. The video was then worked on so that no facial features or body shapes could be seen. The individuals filmed became less than the stick people children draw. All you could see on the video were points of light, which marked the joints of people as they moved.

Skeletal information, you might say.

Subjects were then asked to decide whether the movement of these points of light depicted joy, sadness or some other emotion. A fast, busy exuberant movement would suggest joy to a normal reader of body language. But those who suffered from schizophrenia could not begin to decipher what these movements meant in terms of emotions; the other 'normal' subjects managed that quite well.

A second experiment reinforced this. Subjects looked at film clips of complex social scenes but the actors' faces had been erased. Then the faces were edited back in. Normal people understood the mood of these scenes much better when they could see the faces of the actors. But people with schizophrenia did not do any better when the faces were edited back in.

'The film-clip test showed that patients with schizophrenia have problems both with taking advantage of extra information that is conveyed by the human face and with deciphering socially relevant stimuli that are not conveyed by facial expression,' said psychologist Sergio Paradiso (1999).

People with autism face even worse problems. In his unexpected bestseller, *The Curious Incident of the Dog in the Night-time*, Mark Haddon writes from the point of view of a clever autistic boy. One of the boy's problems is that he takes everything literally. And while he is a genius at logical thinking and doing equations, he simply does not notice or comprehend the most basic aspects of body language, such as that if his mother is crying it means she is sad.

It is not clear why people with mental health problems do not read body language well. But most people can learn. And if this book is to teach you how to observe, there is one skill you need to become a Maestro of Body Language.

How to watch others – discreetly

This requires a basic but cunning technique. Never stare too long at people you are watching (which might upset them) but glance at

Figure 1.7   Watching others discreetly

them from time to time (Figure 1.7). In such situations – and during my research for this book I often watched people – I would turn my head away but keep looking at my 'subjects' out of the corner of my eye. It's a trick worth practising.

2

The basics of body language

Every spoken language from the Queen's English to gangland Japanese breaks down into nouns, verbs, adverbs, adjectives and sentences. Body language also has its basics and grammar. We need to grasp what these are.

Mirroring

I want to start this chapter by looking at something many of us sometimes do – either consciously or unconsciously. Recent research has made some surprising discoveries about how and why we 'mirror'.

Figure 2.1 Mirroring or postural echo

I see you cross your arms and to show I am in sympathy with you I fold my arms too. Sometimes this is called postural echo (Figure 2.1).

Until the late 1970s, psychologists assumed that this ability to mirror was only found in children aged six or older, by which time they could be very deliberate. But then someone stumbled on something extraordinary.

In the 1980s, psychologists were amazed to discover that if they stuck their tongues out at a two-day-old baby, the baby often stuck out his or her tongue back. Newborn babies were supposed to be mere bundles of reflexes who could just about suck at the nipple and excrete. The discovery that they could imitate actions flabbergasted scientists.

Exercise 2.1: Mirroring in babies

If you have a newborn baby or can visit one, stick your tongue out at him or her and see what happens.

The conclusion was clear: newborn babies could pay attention to other people's eyes and faces. Thirty years ago, psychologists did not realize how the brain made this possible. The babies didn't know it, of course, but were 'using' what are now called mirror neurons. They were first discovered, Charles Darwin would have been happy to note, in monkeys.

Monkey see, monkey do – thanks to mirror neurons

Studies of macaque monkeys have found that they have mirror neurons in their frontal lobes, which are above the eyes. The frontal lobes are involved in planning, among other things.

Mirror neurons fire not just when the monkeys perform certain tasks, but also when they watch someone else perform the same task. A similar observation and action-matching system exists in humans. When I see you cross your arms, neural circuits that tell me to cross my own arms start firing in my brain. When you see someone who looks angry, hurt or happy, your mirror neurons activate circuits in the brain for anger, hurt or happiness.

A recent study in Germany by Andreas Hennenlotter (2005) looked at what the brain does when we smile. He used brain imaging to see what was happening both when subjects smiled and when people smiled at them. The neurons that started to fire when someone smiled at them were much the same neurons that fired when subjects themselves smiled.

Enthusiasts claim these neurons help explain how we manage some very surprising skills, including imitation, intuition, empathy and, according to some, mind-reading. Individuals who have sustained damage to their frontal lobes can have many problems with social skills which depend on such abilities.

Exercise 2.2: Self-observation

One evening at home, whether you are with your partner, friends or your parents, mirror every position they assume and gesture they make. If they cross their arms, you cross your arms. If they lean forward, you lean forward.

Do this for 15 minutes and try to keep count of how many of their gestures you mirror. Then ask if they noticed anything odd about your behaviour.

The best answer, of course, is that they did not notice anything. If they did, you are mirroring a little too crudely. You want them to feel you are giving them empathic support but not to realize just how you are doing it.

Some of the other basics of body language are:

Facial expression

The human face is hugely expressive. Often, you do not have to say a word for someone to understand you are sad or happy or frightened. We are good at recognizing six basic emotional expressions – happiness, disgust, sadness, fear, anger and surprise (see Figure 2.4, overleaf).

Normal children can read the meaning of the look on a face from the age of four, if not earlier. By the time they are five years old, they are also quite good fakers; they know how to look happy or sad, even if they don't feel like that (though they tend to exaggerate the expressions a little while learning to deceive.) One could argue that children have to learn this – if we were honest all the time, life would be even more stressful. So our faces don't always reveal what

Happiness

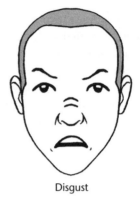

Disgust

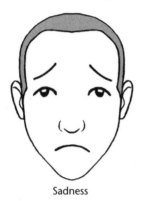

Sadness

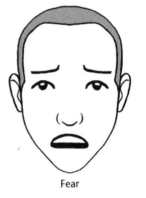

Fear

Anger

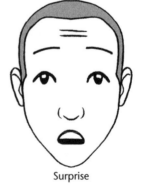

Surprise

Figure 2.2   Six basic facial expressions

we feel. One of the problems children with autism have to cope with is that people find it hard to react to children who always tell the literal truth.

Movements of the head

The average human being nods a hundred times an hour when they are not alone. To nod consciously is usually to say 'yes', but the really interesting nods are those that people don't necessarily notice. These signal, for example, that I am listening to you or that I would like to say something now.

There has also been much research on the origin of head shaking – which seems to mean 'no' in nearly every culture. One suggestion is that when babies have had enough of their mother's milk and no longer want to suck at the nipple, they turn their heads away. It's one of the first actions over which the baby has control, and that is how people learn to shake their heads to say no.

Angle of the body to others

The way a person positions their body to other people is key – it can be open or closed, welcoming or defensive. It has been argued that there are basically eight ways the body can be positioned in relation to other people.

Exercise 2.3: Self-observation

What position do you get into when you are sitting with someone you love?

How does it change if he or she has said something that really annoys you?

Think of the last time you made up with someone – how did your body positions change during the process?

One of the nicest ways to position your body in relation to a lover is to spoon round them or for them to spoon round you. It's no accident that the spoon resembles the foetal position.

Many women psychologists point out that men sprawl and just take up more space than women do. A typical male sitting position is with both knees jutting outwards while women sit more neatly (Figure 2.3).

Figure 2.3   The difference between male and female styles of sitting

Hand gestures

Gestures are used in myriad ways – to emphasize something that is said, or sometimes instead of words. But there are also times when gestures contradict words. For example, if someone says she thinks

Figure 2.4   Hand gestures: tapping

an employee have just done a good piece of work and taps her fingers on the table or, worse, bites her nails, he should watch his back. These are not usually glowing signs of warmth and so they suggest she is being insincere in her praise (Figure 2.4).

The position of the palms is also a critical cue. An open, upturned palm suggests vulnerability – and conveys a very different meaning to a palm which faces down, let alone a clenched fist (Figure 2.5).

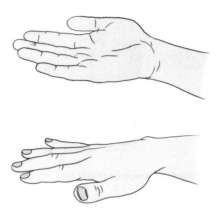

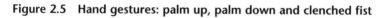

Figure 2.5   Hand gestures: palm up, palm down and clenched fist

Arm gestures and positions

Arm gestures are bigger and cruder than hand gestures.

Many people feel clumsy because they sometimes just don't know what to do with their arms. One solution is the royal one. Prince Charles often either puts his arms behind his back or sticks his hands in his pockets which, of course, means he does not have to worry about what to do with his hands or arms (Figure 2.6, overleaf). But the pose can also suggest you have something to hide.

Figure 2.6   Arm positions: hands in pockets

We often use our arms to include other people, but we can also use them to reject others. The arm round your shoulder says, 'I am with you,' or 'I want to protect you.' If we cross our arms, however, it is a defensive gesture, a barrier which says, 'Do not come near me.'

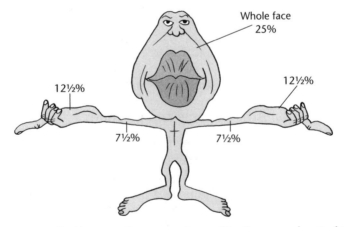

Figure 2.7   The Homunculus: percentage of brain space devoted to parts of the body

Movements of other parts of the body, like knees, ankles and feet, are under less conscious control than movements of the arms and hands. One sign of this is a classic illustration called the Homunculus (Figure 2.7) which shows how much brain space is devoted to different limbs. Notice how much is devoted to the lips, hands and fingers.

Knees, feet and ankles

We are less aware of people looking at these extremities to judge what they feel. Our knees and feet aren't always conveying profound messages but they do often indicate how nervous a person is.

Leaning forward when sitting and clasping both knees with the hands is a form of self-touching, of seeking for comfort. It also means 'I am about to leave,' according to Desmond Morris, the author of *The Naked Ape*. See Figure 2.8.

The following are some very common foot positions people adopt, without necessarily being aware of them:

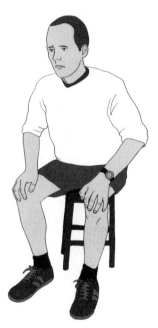

Figure 2.8 The knee clasp

Figure 2.9   The ankle wrap

- The toes are splayed out towards someone else or turned inwards. The first position is essentially an invitation to interact; the second is the opposite – a warning to 'leave you alone'.
- One foot is wrapped around the other ankle (Figure 2.9). This position suggests you are anxious, and are touching yourself partly to counter that anxiety.
- One foot is tapping. This can be a sign of anxiety, but it can also force you to concentrate by building up body tension.

Figure 2.10   Crossed legs

Next time you spot someone with his ankle wrapped round the back of his foot, ask if he remembers when – and why – he did it. He probably won't.

Crossed legs are usually a defensive posture (Figure 2.10) – as are many instances when we touch ourselves. Many of these touches are self-comforting or self-protective. If I am scared, I hug myself. But such gestures can also serve as 'get-alert' signals. People do literally pinch themselves. Mediaeval monks were given to flagellating themselves as a penance, but it also kept them alert.

Gaze and eye contact

The way we look at people is profoundly revealing. Do we stare? Do we look quickly and then look away? How long do we keep looking?

Eye gaze has fascinated people throughout the ages. Sumerian clay tablets dating back to 3000 BC tell how Ereshkigal, goddess of the underworld, had the power to kill Inanna, goddess of love, with the eye of death. Less dramatically, in our day eye contact has been the subject of much research.

Social codes of looking

The six muscles that cooperate to move each of our eyeballs are ancient and common to all vertebrates; the nerves of these muscles are linked to the unconscious as well as to the thinking parts of our brain. So our looks may well sometimes say more than we intend!

Our 'gaze behaviour' – including how long we may look at another person – tends to be regulated by our culture. As a general rule in Western cultures, if you look too little you may be perceived as shifty or deceitful; if you look too much you may be perceived as domineering. We tend to feel comfortable if the other person's gaze meets ours for some 60–70 per cent of the time – more than that, and we create an impression of extra-special interest. Why else do lovers gaze into each other's eyes? If you make eye contact for less than a third of the time you are with someone, however, the person you are with is likely to suspect you have something to hide or that you are dishonest.

Figure 2.11   The dominant stare

In some cultures it is normal for people to indulge in more eye contact than in the West. In Arabia, Latin America and southern Europe – all labelled 'contact' cultures – people tend to look more than the British or white Americans. In such contact cultures, too little gaze is seen as insincere, dishonest or impolite, while in non-contact cultures too much gaze ('staring') can be seen as threatening, disrespectful and insulting (Argyle 1975).

Staring can also be interpreted as a sign of dominance, while looking away or avoiding eye contact may be seen as submissive. This may have evolved from primate behaviour where the unwavering gaze is a dominant ploy. The sociologist Erving Goffman (1989) described one extreme example of this: the sustained 'hate stare'. Those you stare at for too long usually interpret this as not just deliberate, but an aggressive violation of the normal rules of looking (Figure 2.11).

Continuing the theme of dominance in looking – or who has the right to look – some researchers describe the 'colonial' gaze, or 'tourist' gaze, which seems to be a detached, potentially proprietorial way of looking at someone or something you may want to claim. Jonathan Schroeder of the University of Exeter (1998) comments that 'explorers gaze upon newly discovered land as colonial resources'.

Closing your eyes when you speak, or constantly fluttering the eyelids to give a closed-lid effect, is often disconcerting for those who are listening to you (Figure 2.12). It seems that you are shutting the listener out from your consciousness, and may also indicate that you are not telling the truth. You may do this out of habit and are quite likely to be unaware of it, but the impact is very negative. Closing your eyes when you talk to someone is not one of the most sympathetic of eye gestures.

Figure 2.12   The eyelid flutter

At the other end of the scale, attractiveness can be directly related to the size of a person's pupils. Studies have shown that people, especially women, are perceived as more attractive if their pupils are more dilated than normal (Figure 2.13, overleaf). In some cultures, belladonna was and sometimes still is used to enlarge the pupils.

Gaze has also been said to convey sexual orientation. Some gay men claim they can recognize each other by a special gaze, described as 'not only lingering, but also a visual probing' by author Patrick Higgins in his book *A Queer Reader* (1993).

Psychologists regularly film meetings, the way parents and children behave and what people do on first dates, to study what eye contact reveals. Video cameras now make it possible to track

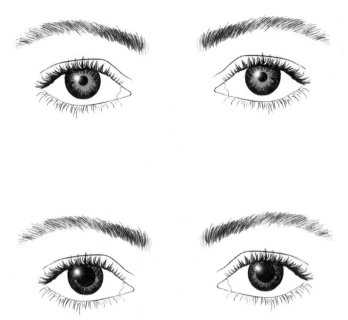

Figure 2.13 The eyes: pupil sizes

minutely where people are looking. And sometimes they look at their own body or parts of it.

Such 'self-gaze' is quite revealing, especially when these looks are very quick, and is quite often unconscious. The looks are signs of anxiety, as if people are checking that they are actually still there and still exist. The conscious look in the mirror is quite different.

Some schools of therapy, like Neuro-Linguistic Programming, claim that where someone looks reveals much about what he or she is thinking – a claim I will examine in Chapter 9.

Tics and displacements

We are often not aware of what we are doing. I think I am gazing intently at you but, at the same time, I'm also scratching my cheek and checking my tie. Both of these are perfectly acceptable but they suggest sometimes underlying anxieties. Women often touch their hair and flick it back (Figure 2.14). Sometimes we become unable to control particular tics and displacement activities, which can become acutely distressing.

And as I've already mentioned, displacement activities are often the result of stress or ambivalence: I pick at the lint on my suit because I am so excited I need to do something; I want to hold your hand but I'm afraid I'll be rejected.

Figure 2.14   A displacement activity: the hair flick

Case history

A good example of displacement activity was given in an interview with Niko Tinbergen, the Nobel prize-winning animal behaviourist. Tinbergen told me:

> When one of my children began to yawn compulsively our family doctor said, 'She seems to be very tired,' and I had to explain to him that she was scared stiff – it is a very common displacement activity such as scratching or biting your nails when under slight stress. (Cohen 1977)

Exercise 2.4: Self-observation

What tics do you have?

Write down six of the things you do when you are anxious.

Ask someone you are close to how many of them they notice.

Do you want to change them? You can – by working out what they are and developing a training routine so that they stop being your normal unconscious responses.

I hope I have made clear that these basics of body language give rise to a dilemma. How do we know someone means what they are saying to us? Or, to put it more poetically,

You're smiling.
I wonder if you mean it
I'm as sure as can be –
you're asking
the same question about me.

My 'poem' is inspired by a book written by R. D. Laing, a famous psychiatrist of the 1960s and 1970s. In *Knots* (1970), he explored the tangle of human relationships in such verses – and returned time and again to the big question:

- How do I know what you are thinking?

And the more self-obsessed ones:

- How do I know what you are thinking about me?
- Am I revealing things through my body language I don't want to reveal?
- If I am revealing anxieties, weaknesses and secret impulses, what can I do to change the way I 'leak' clues? (Leak isn't a very elegant way of putting it. But it is, as we have seen, the jargon psychologists use.)

The question of what someone thinks about you starts the moment you meet them.

3

First impressions

When you walk into a room, what impression you do make? Do people look at you and think: 'There's someone confident'? Or do they think: 'Poor pathetic creature'? Or, worst of all, do they not notice you at all?

In 1979, an American psychologist, Robert Zajonc, published a theory of *hot cognitions*; he claimed that we make almost instant judgements when we encounter new people. Within three seconds of meeting someone new, we decide whether we like them or not. Our response is not so much a rational assessment as something emotional – sometimes we call it chemistry. But what triggers this chemistry is less clear.

Brain research shows how quickly this chemical reaction happens. It takes about 400 milliseconds to trigger a response – either positive or negative! Initially, Zajonc argued there was nothing we could do to affect someone's hot cognitions of us. But that has changed as we have discovered more and more about what creates good and bad first impressions.

Exercise 3.1: Self-observation

You are going out on a date. What do you do?

Does anxiety make you pause, check and re-check yourself?

Do you resent all the trouble you are taking?

Or do you think you look okay as it is – and if he or she likes you, it won't make any difference?

In the past, only women spent much time making up and grooming themselves. But in the last 15 years men have also started to prettify themselves so there is now a large industry devoted to male beauty products. We are endlessly neurotic about our appearance, but luckily there are always experts willing to help.

Image-makers

Michelle T. Sterling founded Global Image Group, which helps 'clients develop a strong first impression and brand identity, through wardrobe and image development, communication, etiquette and protocol skills'. She argues that each and every one of us is a 'brand' and adds:

> People appraise your visual and behavioral appearance from head to toe. They observe your demeanor, mannerisms, and body language and even assess your grooming and accessories – watch, handbag and briefcase. Within only three seconds, you make an indelible impression. You may intrigue some and disenchant others. Once the first impression is made, it is virtually irreversible.

But there is hope, Sterling claims:

> You can learn to make a positive and lasting first impression, modify it to suit any situation, and come out a winner. Doing so requires you to assess and identify your personality, physical appearance, lifestyle and goals.

I don't promise this book will turn you into a global brand, but it should at least make you aware of some of the ways you can go wrong – and help you start to fix your flaws.

Mr Tall conquers all

Consider these two descriptions:

> She walked into the room, her shoulders held high, and smiled.

> He shambled into the room and slumped down on a chair in the far corner.

We form images of these two people quickly – partly because we associate posture with personality and self-confidence.

The first element of 'good' body language has been known for centuries. In ancient Rome, soldiers were taught to stand up and stand tall. If you slouched on your spear, the centurion yelled at you just as the drill sergeant will today, 2,000 years later.

The idea that standing tall conveys self-confidence, poise and good character is deeply ingrained in human beings. It comes from our animal heritage. The animal who stands tallest in a pack is often the leader of that pack.

Men are very aware of their own height and may fret about it because they believe women prefer men who are above average height. In November 2006 a quick trawl of the Lonely Hearts in the *Sunday Telegraph* showed that the first word men used most often to describe themselves was not sexy or intelligent or charming but TALL.

The same was true in *The Times* of 17 November 2006. Twelve of the 39 men who were looking for women said they were tall, tall and good-looking, tall and interesting or tall and solvent. Tall is all.

Until recently, short men were stuck. Few things look as silly as men who wear shoes with high heels – but now new shoe technology offers hope. On the internet you can buy

Figure 3.1 A confident person

height-increase insoles or individually made status shoes. No one can spot they're giving you a lift. These force you to walk on tiptoe and can increase your height by between 8 and 10 cm. But if you don't want to mess about with fancy shoes, at least make sure you stand tall and straight.

When a confident person enters the room, he or she looks around to size up the situation (Figure 3.1, page 35). Socially skilled individuals pause briefly and head in a definite direction. They are then adept at inserting themselves into a group without appearing to be barging in.

Decide which group you are going to make for. Once you have made that decision, don't waver.

Spot a gap between people where you can fit yourself in. If there is no obvious gap, hover on the edge of the group. Place your feet so that they are gently nudging in. You can then gradually introduce yourself into the circle. This can be done in two ways:

1 without saying a word, by leaning in with one shoulder and moving your feet (Figure 3.2).
2 by saying something to announce your presence; the group then has to be quite rude to reject you.

Figure 3.2 Joining a conversation

It is much harder to insert yourself into a group if your posture lacks confidence because you will not nudge your shoulders and feet so easily into the circle.

> **Tip**
>
> If you feel unsure about how to do this, you can practise it with one or two friends; the art of inserting your shoulders is a subtle one.

The most solid finding is simple and not surprising. Someone who stands looks more dominant than someone who is sitting. Height really matters, but so does the way you sit.

The man in Figure 3.3 is sitting hunched into himself and does not look out or at anyone. The posture suggests depression and lack of confidence.

Figure 3.3   A posture suggesting lack of confidence

Sometimes, however, posture can scream that someone is an over-confident layabout. The man who has put his feet up on his desk almost certainly has an inflated ego and is very possessive of his territory. That pose says, 'I own it all and I don't care how rude it looks.' Don't do it. And be on your guard against anyone who does, and of the slightly less offensive soul who drapes his leg over a chair when talking to you.

To test how good your posture is you have to be prepared to be self-critical in the mirror.

Exercise 3.2: Self-observation – the 'look-in-the-mirror' test

Strip down to your underwear. Stand in front of a large mirror.

- Breathe deeply. Close your eyes. Count to ten. Open your eyes.
- Focus on yourself in the mirror.
- The first thing you have to work out is: are you standing straight? Turn and look at yourself in profile, as that is the best position in which to judge how straight you are standing.
- Watch for the angle of your head. Is it held high or is it inclined, sloping down to your shoulders? If it's sloping down, stretch it back till it is straight.
- An acid test of how straight you stand sounds like something out of ballet school: place a book on your head. Does it fall off at once? Or can you, first, just keep it balanced on your head standing still? If you can do that, then try walking two steps, then five steps, without the book falling off.

If you can manage five steps without the book falling off, you really are standing straight.

> **Tip**
>
> If you are in a relationship, you can observe each other – and time which of you can keep a book on their head longer.
>
> But don't try this with anything heavy. A friend of mine tried carrying a container of water on her head after seeing a film on women in Africa, where they do this all the time. She put her back out and needed physiotherapy for nine months. Stick to books.

Posture helps create Zajonc's hot cognitions (1979). Someone who slouches is seen as less confident, and depressed people tend to slouch more. Standing tall won't just make you look good, it will also make you feel good. The science-fiction writer Brian Aldiss, writing in *The Times* to celebrate his 80th birthday in 2005, said he still liked to walk tall when he went to his local shops. It always improved his mood.

Sometimes men and women add to their height by the way they style their hair.

The Big Hair look

In mammals generally, clean hair is a sign of high status, good health and careful grooming. As birds preen their feathers and lions puff their mane, so humans use hair as part of their display.

People have been doing so for thousands of years. Upper-class women in the Egyptian Middle Kingdom liked huge wigs and bound their tresses with ribbons of silver or linen which they then topped with jewellery. The French queen, Marie Antoinette pioneered the bouffant hairdo. Punk hair is less bouffant but even more colourful and, in its way, big.

Psychologists have found that women mark lifestyle and career changes with different hairstyles, according to Grant McCracken in his 1997 book, *Big Hair: A Journey into the Transformation of Self*. Your hair also signals some aspects of your personality, according to a Procter & Gamble study by Marianne LaFrance of Yale in 2000. She found that, in the USA at least, hairstyle plays a significant role in first impressions. For a woman, short, tousled hair conveys confidence and an outgoing personality, but does not suggest she is sexy. A medium-length, casual haircut suggests intelligence and good nature; while long, straight, blonde hair projects sexuality and affluence. And letting your roots show is seen as a sign of depression.

> **Tip**
>
> If you feel low, get your hair done – and your nails.

The next hurdle in the first impression stakes is how you greet someone.

Greetings, handshakes and social kissing

Watch people arriving at any function: after the host and the various guests have embraced, they back off and one or both always looks away. Anthropologist Adam Kendon (1994) calls this 'the cut-off' and thinks it may be an equilibrium-maintaining device, as does F. Davis:

> Every relationship except a very new one has its own customary level of intimacy, and if a greeting is more intimate than the relationship warrants, some kind of cut-off is needed afterwards so that everything can quickly get back to normal.
>
> (Davis 1971: 46)

One theory claims that the first people to shake hands were the tribes of the Yemen at the southern tip of the Arabian Peninsula. As Islam spread, the practice grew. In the New Testament, however, St Paul mentions in Galatians that when he visited Jerusalem and met with James, Cephas (Peter) and John, they each gave him 'the right hand of friendship'. If the Bible is right about body language, that would suggest Greek and Roman citizens were shaking hands in order to bond long before Islam started.

Another theory claims men shook hands because they could not 'shake' if they were carrying a sword, dagger or gun. In the Middle Ages, when knights were always rapiering each other, offering your open hand showed you came in peace and were not concealing a weapon (Figure 3.4).

Figure 3.4 Two knights shake hands

But whenever the handshake started, it appears to have gone out of fashion by 1660. In 1662 the diarist Samuel Pepys wrote as if hand-shaking were a new-fangled custom. His entry for Saturday 15 February 1662 runs:

With the two Sir Williams to the Trinity-house; and there in their society had the business debated of Sir Nicholas Crisp's house at Deptford. Then to dinner and after dinner I was sworn a Younger Brother; Sir W. Rider being Deputy Master for my Lord of Sandwich; and after I was sworn, all the Elder Brothers shake me by the hand: it is their custom, it seems.

If it was 'their custom, it seems', shaking hands could hardly have been that common.

The Quakers also introduced the handshake among themselves around 1660, as they felt it was more egalitarian and less flowery than the then usual bowings, scrapings and salaams. The second American president, Thomas Jefferson, who entered the White House in 1797, encouraged shaking hands for similar reasons.

The good shake

Today the handshake is a universal gesture from Tokyo to Tottenham. The Japanese used to bow to introduce themselves, but as they have become increasingly Westernized, they shake hands more. But shaking hands is not as simple as it seems, because the wrong shake suggests a flawed personality.

Caudillo (2002), a psychologist who has made the handshake her life study, argues that if you proffer a limp handshake you are likely to be seen as insecure and untrustworthy. Those who give a full, firm handshake (Figure 3.5a, overleaf) will be judged to be more out-going, more open to new experiences, more conscientious and more agreeable. Women who shake firmly get rated as more intelligent.

Caudillo stresses, for example, that nurses must know how to shake hands well, both to reassure patients and to establish their own professional status. A good shake also requires steady eye contact. You should look the person you are shaking with straight in the eyes, though without staring too hard at them.

Exercise 3.3: Self-observation

Write down what you find off-putting when someone shakes hands with you.

When shaking hands, the position of the palm reveals a great deal about the different status of the shakers. In Figure 3.5 (b), the top

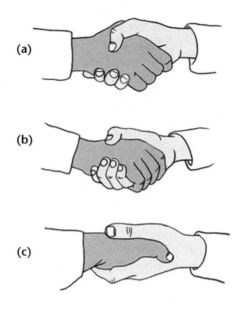

Figure 3.5   Different types of handshake

palm clamps down on the other one. This is the position of power. In Figure 3.5 (c), the man is exposing the 'vulnerable' inside of his palm.

The infamous Nazi salute was palm down, and signalled their obsession with power and control. A complete opposite is Roderick Spode, a ludicrous would-be dictator invented by the English comic writer P. G. Wodehouse. Spode fails totally as a leader. And what is his movement's salute? The Spode salute has the palm pointed up – not down. No one who wants to be seen as a strong man should place his palms in a position where someone else can slap him down.

The 'high fives' greeting is interesting, as both parties keep their palms vertical so no one dominates.

There are other traps to avoid. Caudillo (2002) warns against a two-handed shake; using the other hand to cover the clasped hands may be meant as friendly, but this can be misconstrued as 'motherly, controlling, or too intimate'. One exception to this rule, however, is when there is a big gap in status between those shaking hands. Bill Clinton is famous for clasping both hands over those he shakes with, and that is always seen as a sign that he cares for 'ordinary' people. People felt flattered if the President of the United States lingered in physical contact with them. But if someone 'normal' puts his free hand on the other person's shoulders or grips their forearms, he is invading the other person's 'personal space', which may be resented.

In an amusing aside, Caudillo advises people who suffer from sweaty palms to keep a handkerchief handy and dry their hands just before shaking.

The question of how long to keep shaking is also the subject of research. Let go too soon and that suggests you think the other person's hand is dirty and that you don't want to be shaking it anyway. Cling on for too long, and you seem to be invading the other person's space. The perfect length of time to hold on to the other person's hand is 2.7 seconds, according to Caudillo.

Greetings and personality

Your movements also give an impression of your personality. People who make strong, definite movements are seen as more dominant. We also see people as more dominant if they gesticulate more, make more eye contact and show more animation on their face. Table 3.1 shows this clearly.

Table 3.1 Differences between dominant and submissive people

To look dominant	To look weak
Make definite moves	Wear more clothes!
Make these moves forceful	Make smaller gestures
Keep eye contact	More hand and ankle gestures
Animation on the face	Lack of expression

Submissive women also tend to stay in the same posture for longer while women who move more are seen as dominant.

Exercise 3.4: Self-observation

Time your handshake. If you discover it's too brief, it may reflect your anxiety. Practise till you automatically do it for about 2.7 seconds.

Next, if you want to seem stronger, practise making more dramatic gestures and, especially, swinging the lower part of your leg – though the police have often claimed that the tension of being under suspicion leads guilty people to fidget and swing the lower part of their leg.

But personality is not just a question of how strong or weak your handshake makes you seem.

The British psychologist Hans Eysenck (1973) argued that people could be placed on a continuum of extroversion and introversion. He developed the Eysenck Personality Inventory, which includes questions like:

- Do you enjoy going to parties?
- Do you sometimes feel depressed for no apparent reason?
- Are you usually the person who first touches someone else?

The Eysenck Personality Inventory has proved itself reliable over 40 years. Many of us can be labelled as either extroverts or introverts. And there are significant differences between the two. Introverts are shyer and more anxious; they do not go about slapping people on the back because they are more inhibited about physical contact.

If you are introverted, you probably

1 won't be the first person to offer your hand;
2 will allow someone to place her palm on top of yours;
3 will want to remove your hand first because the contact feels too invasive;
4 will worry about whether your handshake is firm enough.

Extroverts, on the other hand, will not have such self-doubts but may behave in other off-putting ways. For example, they may pump your hand up and down and not let go for well over Caudillo's 'perfect' 2.7 seconds.

Exercise 3.5: Self-observation

To know whether you are introverted or extroverted, look at the following 16 questions. Circle the answer that is most like you.

1 Are you happiest when you get involved in some project that calls for immediate action?

    Yes   Maybe   No

2 When you climb up any stairs, do you normally take them two at a time?

    Yes   No   Maybe

3 Do you eat so fast you usually finish your meal before everyone else?

    Yes   No   Maybe

4 Does slow traffic drive you crazy when you are driving?

    Yes   No   Maybe

5 Do you like setting up leisure activities?

    Yes   Maybe   No

6 You are presented with a new project. Are you likely to feel you really hate having to handle something new?

    Yes   Maybe   No

7 When you are walking with other people, do they often have difficulty keeping up with you?

    No   Yes   Maybe

8 Do you often rush helter-skelter from one activity to another without stopping to relax?

    Yes   Maybe   No

9 Do you often feel you can't be bothered to do things?

    Maybe   No   Yes

10 When you have to meet new people, do you dread the awful introduction rituals?

    No   Yes   Maybe

11 Is a dreadful holiday one where every day you have to go out to admire some new sight no tourist could miss?

    No   Yes   Maybe

12 Do you find that you are often anxious for no reason?

    No   Yes   Maybe

13 Do you usually wake up in the morning bright and raring to go?

    Yes   Maybe   No

14 Do other people seem to you to be more outgoing than you are?

   Yes   Maybe   No

15 If they seem more outgoing, does that make you feel worried?

   No   Yes   Maybe

16 Do you get agitated if you have to wait for someone?

   Yes   Sometimes   No

Answers

Extroverts will answer Yes to Questions 1, 2, 3, 4, 5, 7, 8 and 13.

Introverts will answer Yes to Questions 6, 9, 10, 11, 12, 14, 15 and 16.

- So score 2E for each Yes to the extrovert questions and 1E for each Maybe.
- Score 2N for each Yes to the introvert questions and 1E for each Maybe.
- The highest extrovert score will be 16.
- The highest introvert score is also 16.
- If you score above 10 you are highly extroverted or introverted.
- In the range 6–10 you are middling.
- In the range 0–4 your scores are low.
- It is unlikely but not impossible for someone to score high on both extroversion and introversion. Such people will gladhand others and behave in a very confident and expansive way but they will also feel anxious about that very behaviour. It may feel like an act to them and their body language may well veer from one extreme to another, so if you are like that, learning to relax and slow down might be sensible.

Social kissing

In elegant society, men used to kiss the fingers of women rather than shake their hands. But now in the UK when men and women, and women and women, meet, they often kiss, especially if they are middle class. These aren't passionate kisses but air kisses and skin rarely meets skin; sometimes there may be a light brush of the lips on the cheek.

The sexes started to kiss socially as far back as the 1920s, the era of jazz and big dance bands. Conservatives feared this would lead to unbridled orgies, so everyone had to buckle up and restrain themselves. The best way was to kiss but not really kiss, which is a good definition of social kissing. Putting your lips briefly to someone's cheek is intimate but, in theory at least, not sexual.

In the *Boston Globe* in September 2006, writer Daniel Akst warned, however, that; 'Kissing hello and goodbye is surely more dangerous than a handshake, and the whole cheek-to-cheek pecking business can become dreadfully embarrassing.'

Akst added,

At dinner parties, I come away from this uneasy minuet feeling that I've somehow mishandled things or been slighted. A social triple lutz for men and women alike, the whole complex negotiation is a perfect metaphor for the exquisite dance of self-mastery all of us must perform in our relentlessly coed, multi-ethnic, and hypersensitive society. It's a test, in other words.

I suspect that Akst hates social kissing partly because he is quite introverted.

The test for the social kisser is to show you can get close without getting intimate. After all, you social kiss in public, not in the privacy of your bedroom. 'It reflects the need to seem natural and unconstrained at all times,' Akst noted, 'even though of course one's lack of constraint is itself entirely constrained (which is why we have social kissing rather than social fondling).'

Akst argued that social kissing is 'a social safety valve'. He said, perhaps a little dramatically, that it is 'regulated infidelity – kind of like bundling among the Puritans, except designed to inoculate against courtship rather than promote it'. Bundling was the practice whereby young unmarried Puritans shared a bed but were not supposed to touch; they were put in an intimate situation, but no intimacy was supposed to take place because the Bible forbade it.

Akst noted,

Humans weren't made to spend this much time in the company of members of the opposite sex who aren't our spouses, who get dolled up before coming to the office, and who inevitably develop some level of intimacy with us. People need some socially sanctioned system of building immunity toward one another.

And social kissing provides such a system because it has strict rules. When we meet people of the opposite sex in our free and easy, if stressed, society, we often have the maximum of temptation and the maximum of opportunity. So we need boundaries – and the rules of social kissing provide those.

When you kiss romantically, you look into someone's eyes. When you greet someone with a social kiss, you usually end up looking at his or her ear (Figure 3.6).

Figure 3.6 Social kissing

Tips

It is wise, therefore, to follow these rules.

1 Do not social kiss on the lips.
2 The kiss should be quick. A kiss on the cheek of more than 1.5 seconds suggests that one of you at least has a more intimate agenda in mind.
3 Do not lean your body into the other person's body – which is what you would do in a normal kiss.
4 Do not put your arms around the person you are social kissing. That is too forceful.
5 Do not kiss them on the nose as this is too playful and intimate.
6 If you are air-kissing be sure not to nibble the ear!

You may now practise social kissing with whoever you like!

Gang body language

Studies of body language also stress the differences between different cultures, as we shall see in Chapter 11. The principle also applies to particular sub-cultures.

Standing ramrod straight is not the way to show that you are confident in certain social groups. The gangs of Peckham – and indeed of Moscow – aren't known for their military posture but they have their own body language and swaggers for conveying confidence.

In the next chapter I look at personal space and how we can use body language to define and defend it.

4

Personal space and the personal touch

You know the feeling when you are at a party. Jim has had a little too much to drink and is telling you how the world really is. To make sure you don't miss a syllable of his wisdom, he leans right into your face. You can see every mark on his skin.

When a man is 'right in your face' or 'too much in your face' – this is usually an aggressive gesture (Figure 4.1).

Figure 4.1 'In your face'

Personal space is the invisible area around each of us, the space we feel we need to keep others out of in order to be comfortable – the very centre of our territory. But if someone comes into our personal space it does not always have to be uncomfortable.

One of the great clichés of cinema is the close-up before the first kiss. In the film *The American President* Michael Douglas plays a widowed president who invites a political lobbyist, played by Annette Bening, to dinner. As they inspect the china in the White House he comes closer to her.

She comes closer to him.

They edge into each other's personal space.

Their moves are tentative – but their hormones are in overdrive.

Then their faces and lips move closer to each other.

Then the personal space between them dissolves as they kiss … At this romantic moment an aide interrupts: the President is needed in the Situation Room to decide whether or not to bomb Libya.

Eventually, though, the romance gets back on track. A frame-by-frame analysis of the seconds leading up to the kiss shows clearly

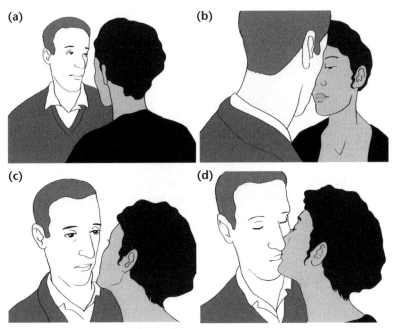

Figure 4.2   A frame-by-frame kiss

the way we can let someone into the personal space we usually protect (Figure 4.2).

The extent of personal space

Psychologists have tried to measure the personal space or 'bubble' we create around ourselves. The best estimate – and it is an estimate – is that for an average Westerner personal physical space is about 60 cm on either side, 70 cm in front and 40 cm behind. Culture and personality both affect what people see as comfortable personal space – culture more so.

Some researchers claim that there are four categories of personal space:

1 the intimate distance for embracing or whispering (15–45 cm);
2 the personal distance for conversations among good friends (45–120 cm);
3 the social distance for conversations among acquaintances (120–360 cm);
4 the public distance used for public speaking (360 cm or more).

Exercise 4.1: Self-observation

Try to work out your comfortable personal space. To do this, you need to stand close to:

● a good friend;
● someone you are having a relationship with;
● a work colleague;
● (if you are a parent) one of your children.

Note the differences in how close you are with these different groups – and especially when you feel too close for comfort.

This can be turned into a good party game.

The boundaries of personal space depend not just on culture but also on circumstances.

I often travel on the London tube in the rush hour when everyone is crammed up against perfect strangers. Normally you would only be this near to someone in an intimate situation. Forced so close

Figure 4.3   'Keep-out' signals

to people like this, we use many conscious and unconscious signals to remind ourselves, and our fellow travellers, that this is not true closeness (Figure 4.3). There is no reason to suppose the Paris, Athens, Moscow, New York or Tokyo tubes are any different.

'Keep out even though you are so close' signals

- One way people cope with so much proximity is to turn the trunk away so that while they stay physically close, that closeness is less direct.
- Avoiding eye contact is another 'keep-out' signal. The glassy stare at no one makes it very clear they are not inviting real involvement. The eyes almost defocus in this situation.
- Avoiding speech is another such signal: not speaking to anyone even though they have a perfect view of the other person's eyes, hair and – sometimes – dandruff.
- A fourth signal is the way passengers avoid any touch even if other people are only an inch away. This sometimes requires a few contortions.

If people do accidentally touch, they tend to apologize with a quick, terse 'sorry'. The tension such closeness causes becomes obvious if the train jolts to a halt and people bump into each other. Passengers burst into nervous laughter. They have been in a situation which seems to be intimate but have just avoided touching each other. Now the train has banged them together and the nervous laughter is both a release and a signal that makes it clear touching other travellers is a mistake. Children often burst out laughing when they make mistakes, but because their body language is less assured they also often add something like 'Oops, I shouldn't have done that.'

Some psychologists argue that passengers on the underground do not see each other as individuals but as inanimate objects, and that this is the only way we avoid fights and mad passionate clinches between London Bridge and Piccadilly. I find this a bit extreme. People know perfectly well that their fellow sardines on the tube are human beings just like them, and understand that it's only the fact they are all travelling on the crowded train that pushes them so physically close.

But again, there are issues of personality. Extroverts will tend to have fewer inhibitions about invading personal space. Introverts will be more awkward about allowing people into their personal space – and need more of it. Men who are seen as cold seem to be given more space, too.

A well-established personality test, the Myers-Briggs Type Indicator, even claims there is a kind of personality – the 'I never get perfection type' – who may have a more extreme need for personal space than others. People with this personality type feel deeply and hate conflict, which is why they hate having their personal space invaded.

Personal space and territory

Changing the distance between two people can also signal an increase or decrease in dominance. I get close to you to emphasize a point I want to make, and often it can be one you don't want to hear.

Police interrogators are taught that this 'violation' of personal space can put pressure on suspects and witnesses. Detectives crowd the person they are interrogating. Such invasion of personal space gives the interrogator a psychological advantage. In a film I made for Channel 4, *The False Confessions File* (1990), a number of suspects described how pressured they felt when officers came very close to them.

The idea of personal space is linked to that of territory. Humans do not mark their territories as animals do by urinating, but the principle is much the same. People vary in how territorial they are, but to be highly territorial is very human. It is a trait we have inherited from other animals – and you can see that at lectures, on planes and in your own home. Students who attend the second in a series of lectures usually sit in precisely the same seats they occupied at the first lecture. People do their best in trains and planes to make sure the seat next to them stays empty; they often pile it with coats and luggage.

A teenager may well see his or her room as private territory and ban Mum and Dad from coming in. Often men make their study or the garden shed their sacred space. There are no serious studies of whether men are more territorial than women, but I have been in relationships where if I trespassed into a woman's dressing space or the table where she kept her make-up, there would be hell to pay.

The quiz in Exercise 4.2 may not reveal the most flattering aspects of your personality, but try to be honest.

Exercise 4.2: Self-observation – how territorial are you?

Which of the following statements is true of you? Again we will use a five-point scale:

5 Always true
4 Quite often true
3 Sometimes true
2 Very occasionally true
1 Absolutely untrue

1 I like my house to be neat and tidy.
2 If I can't find something, I always suspect that my other half or the kids have fiddled with it and lost it.
3 When someone sits in my mum's favourite armchair, I get very tense because no one should be using something that was hers.
4 I would always share a toothbrush with my lover.
5 I hate it when the neighbours prune the trees which hang over into our garden.
6 One of the best things about my new job is that I have a parking space of my own.

7   I do not think other people are watching me. That would be really paranoid.

8   On the beach I like to choose the sun-lounger at the end of any section as this gives me more privacy.

9   When someone steps behind my desk at work it doesn't bother me much.

10 I always like to sleep on the same side of the bed.

11 My girlfriend and I take it in turns to drink when we go out. I don't mind her driving me.

12 When I go shopping with my other half, I find it very irritating that he/she thinks that he/she should push the trolley.

13 I have special places where I live where no one else should go.

14 When it comes to decorating the place I live in, I am quite happy to let someone else choose the wallpaper.

15 I know if someone shows signs of moving in on my personal space.

Answers

First, tot up your scores for Questions 1, 2, 3, 5, 6, 8, 9, 10, 12, 13 and 15 (Questions 4, 7, 11 and 14 are different, so leave them for the moment). The total could be 55. If you score between 40 and 55, you are very territorial. If you score between 25 and 40 you are quite territorial. Under 25 makes you very much a free spirit who is not too bothered about what is yours.

For Questions 4, 7, 11 and 14 the answers go the other way – just to keep readers on their toes. If you said 'always' to 14, for example, it would mean that you were not very territorial. So a high score of 20 on these four questions would mean you are not territorial at all. A low score would mean that you are very territorial.

Try to recall if you have recently had a serious argument with someone because you thought they trespassed into your space. What triggered it?

The invasion of personal space

As our sense of personal space is both conscious and unconscious, we use many ways of moving to signal whether we want – or don't want – someone to cross the boundary and come inside.

'Cross into my space' signs

- Little movements of the body which open up the stance.
- Little turns of the face to really look into someone's eyes.
- Physically inching closer together.
- Moving from a closed stance (Figure 4.4a) to an open one (Figure 4.4b).

It is also wise to recognize signs that mean the opposite.

(a)   **(b)**

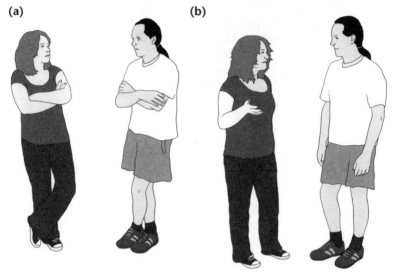

Figure 4.4   'Cross into my personal space'

Definite 'Do not cross into my personal space' signals

- Turning the body away.
- Crossing the arms in front of the body (Figure 4.5, overleaf).
- Retreating movements.
- The elbow pointing like a shield at someone else.
- Putting the arms in front of the face.

One study found that when we feel our personal space is invaded, we also *rub our faces*. The question of personal space is intimately linked to that of touch.

Figure 4.5   'Do not cross into my personal space'

Touch

We are born able to feel pain and pleasure, and as we grow up this sense develops. One reason why we are so sensitive to touch is that the skin is the largest organ of the human body. What do you think it weighs?

The answer is that 15 per cent of our body weight is made up of the skin. The skin of the average adult covers between 1.5–2.0 sq m; most of it is between 2 and 3 mm thick. The average 2.5 sq cm holds 650 sweat glands, 20 blood vessels and more than 1,000 nerve endings or touch receptors. These touch receptors react to pressure – which is what touch fundamentally is – and fire messages to the brain. Put simply, the pattern of that firing 'tells' the brain that a particular touch feels good, bad or neutral.

Most of us have experienced feeling our body hair tingle and even stand on end. This is caused by a rise in something called the galvanic – or electrical – skin response.

Scientists have found that when we are emotionally aroused, our skin is – and feels – more electric. They can measure this, showing that fear, anger, being startled and sexual feelings all produce peaks in the galvanic skin response. In college students, it peaks when a member of the opposite sex comes close to them.

No hugs, please – we're British

In 2006, the headmaster of a British school complained that his pupils were too inclined to hug each other. His attitude illustrates neatly the idea that Brits tend to be very different from Latins, who are always touching each other. The anti-hug head announced a ban on touching on school premises, for which he was mocked in the press.

Different cultures have different-sized personal space 'bubbles', though psychologists disagree about how touchy-feely different nations are. Many people say Americans are more physical, more likely to hug or slap you on the shoulders than British people, but some American research actually questions this stereotype and claims Americans worry about touch. There is little debate about the Japanese or the Arabs, however. The Japanese hardly ever touch while Arabs touch all the time, as we shall see in Chapter 11.

Exercise 4.3: Self-observation

Write down what kind of touch

- you like;
- you dislike;
- you find erotic;
- you find frightening.

In the next chapter I look in detail at some aspects of how we use our arms, hands and feet to reveal – and conceal – what we are really thinking and feeling.

5

Body language's telling little details

Body language can be a matter of life and death. When gladiators fought the lions in ancient Rome, the Emperor could decide whether to let them live or let them die. There were no tannoy systems in 50 BC so how did Caesar let the crowd know?

Thumbs up meant 'Let the gladiator live.'

Thumbs down meant the gladiator was to die.

We still use thumbs up and down to let people know if things have gone well or badly. But we've adopted the gladiator's perspective: thumbs down is bad.

More recently, and more shockingly, survivors of the Nazi concentration camps, like the writer Primo Levi (2000), have described how they tried desperately hard to walk straight when they were being inspected. If you looked fit, you were less likely to be sent to the gas chambers that day.

Body language is not at all trivial.

A chapter in a book cannot explain every move you make, let alone every breath you take. But it can look at the main components of body language in more detail, so I examine:

- body alignment and angular distance;
- hands and fingers;
- arms;
- feet and toes;
- 'puffing up';
- head and shoulders;
- lips;
- self-touch;
- accessories.

Body alignment and angular distance

The way someone lines up the body towards anyone close to them physically – sometimes called the angular distance – is telling. People align the upper body towards those they like and away from those they dislike or are anxious about. Angular distance may range from 0 degrees (*directly facing*) to 180 degrees (*turning one's back*). In the 1960s, body language experts described eight basic orientations of one person towards another person, all based on how they manipulated the space around them. The most intimate is when people gaze at each other; the most disdainful and hostile is when they turn their backs on the people they are with.

Orientation is also a guide to status. You can often work out who is the most powerful person at a conference table by the number of torsos aimed in his, or her, direction. The lesser chickens in the executive pecking order may look at their colleagues when they speak, but their torsos will be mostly turned to the boss – and even more so if they admire her or him.

Nervous people may also swing their bodies away from people (Figure 5.1). President Richard Nixon, the only American president who ever had to resign, used to place himself at an exaggerated angle away from visitors to the Oval Office. White House photographs of meetings in the 1970s show Nixon sitting with his shoulders turned

Figure 5.1 **Swinging away from others**

away from his advisors at 90 degrees, as if to 'remove' himself from everyone else.

Where we place our bodies also affects what we do with our hands.

Hands and fingers

We have seen that a huge amount of brain space is dedicated to the hands (p. **24**) – and that is because hands help to create our intelligence.

When babies are born, they can *grasp* objects. But this is just a reflex. Within a few weeks, they have developed eye–hand co-ordination and can reach for objects in front of them. By the age of four to five months, they use this ability to discover what their world is like. A familiar game is for the baby to pick something up, then drop it, then wait for mummy or daddy to pick it up and put the object back in the baby's hands. The great French child psychologist, Jean Piaget (1896–1980), argued that this apparently silly game of reach and drop is the way we start to make sense of the world. As the baby explores with its hands, it begins to develop what Piaget (1952) called sensori-motor intelligence, which is the root of all intelligence.

By nine months to a year, babies point at things, the first sign of meaningful communication they master. It's one that stays with people for the rest of their lives. We point at things we want to buy, and less-than-subtle men point at girls they fancy.

An interesting variation of pointing is thumbing your nose: putting your hand to your nose, pointing outwards with your thumb and wiggling your fingers. I rather like this gesture, which means 'Ho ho!' It again shows what a strange organ the nose is in terms of body language. The last time I did this was after a young woman asked me if the T-shirt I was wearing meant I was going back into grunge – she thought I was too old for that. I responded by thumbing my nose.

'That is so childish,' Belinda laughed. She was right – but it still made the point. Incidentally, neither of us realized that eighteenth-century Italians used this gesture a great deal.

The nose touch when we lie also helps to conceal an increase of blood flow to the nose, a kind of nasal blushing, so it is a displacement activity which stems from our unconscious awareness of how we show traces of lying on the nose.

Many subtler hand gestures conceal more delicate kinds of ambivalence.

Palms

When a mother puts her hand around a child it's a sign of love – but also of control and comfort. Anthropologists have seen a Ghanaian tribal elder *beat his palm down* to convince listeners that his wives *did* prefer polygamy. (See Figure 5.2b.)

(a)   (b)

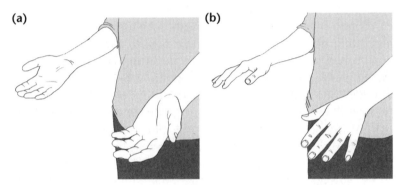

Figure 5.2 Palms up and palms down

To have the palms up, however, is a gesture of helplessness and resignation. When you see someone do this, you might be tempted to the stick the following words in their mouths: 'Heaven help me! I am dealing with someone very silly here!'

Palms also betray anxiety, because they can sweat and become moist. The first director of the FBI, J. Edgar Hoover, never hired any agents whose handshakes were moist because he felt that they would lack moral, as well as manual, grip.

There are a number of other common palm gestures – and two are linked to prayer. When we pray we lace our fingers and sometimes we form a steeple so that our fingers point straight to Heaven (Figure 5.3, overleaf). But these aren't just signs of faith. Both these gestures often lead to small movements that betray anxiety. Many of us also start to tap our fingers against each other or to twist our fingers in our laced hands.

Figure 5.3   Lacing and steepling the fingers

If you tend to do this, practise relaxing your fingers so they don't fidget. If you struggle to do that, put your hands behind your back because it will then be much less noticeable.

We also sometimes sit on our hands, which means, in effect, we are sitting on your palms. Next time you do this check whether your palms are up or down. If you are sitting on your upwardly facing palms, this suggests you are trying to hide your feelings of vulnerability. If you are sitting on the backs of your hands, that is, with down-facing palms, you are probably angry and want to control the person you are talking to, but think (perhaps unconsciously) that you had better not show how livid you are. By sitting on your palms you suppress some of your anger.

You also often see people lace their fingers one by one and touch them, even caress them a little. Again, it's a sign of anxiety and an attempt to soothe ourselves.

Arms

Many people just don't know what to do with their arms and so end up in what seems a tangle of nerves.

The arm cross

People cross their arms defensively all over the world. Women tend to use this gesture when they are with men they do not like or with a man who is making them angry. With arms and elbows pulled tightly into the body, the arm cross suggests *acute nervousness* or *chronic anxiety*. The arm cross can almost become a self-hug which, like all self-touch, is an attempt at self-comfort. You would like someone to hug you to make you feel better but since no one is there or no one will do it, you have to hug yourself.

But when the arms are pressed less tightly against the chest, with elbows held high and away from the body, the arm cross is less a cry for a help and more a wary stance. You are on guard.

Usually we cross our arms in front of our chest (Figure 5.4), but men sometimes also cross their hands in front of their crotch (Figure 5.5, overleaf). One situation where this has been observed is when men are crowded together.

Figure 5.4   The classic arm cross

Hands on hips

With our hands on our hips, we are ready to take charge and trumpet that we are not going to be messed around with. The police take this posture seriously as a warning sign that someone is proud to be anti-social. We don't know whether this 'gunslinger' pose predates our fascination with the Wild West or whether it has sneaked its way into our body language through 1,001 Westerns in which the cowboy puts his hands on his hips before drawing his gun (Figure 5.6).

Figure 5.5   The low hand cross

Figure 5.6   Hands on hips: the 'gunslinger' pose

Case history

Two observations by law-enforcement officers show that they often worry when they see people adopt the gunslinger pose. An FBI agent, Joe Navarro, said, 'It is a territorial-claiming gesture usually present when something is wrong. I don't recommend that officers responding to domestic situations stand in doorways with arms akimbo. They are blocking the king's castle, they are being territorial, and it is a hostile statement when defusion is needed instead. On the other hand, I encourage female officers to use arms akimbo more often to establish greater territory, and thus greater authority.' Another officer argues that he always felt on guard seeing someone in this pose and that he recalled one case where he was questioning a suspect who had one hand on his hip.

Another policeman told psychologists in Los Angeles about an occasion where he thought he was making headway when talking to a suspect. But the hands on hip gesture 'was actually helping him not confess. I finally realized what was going on – so I broke his stance by dropping my pen. Shortly after he picked up my (conveniently) dropped pen, he confessed'.

If someone faces you hands on hips, take a look at his feet. Are they planted firmly on the ground or fidgeting? If you are looking at calm, firm feet, duck for cover. Either verbally or physically, the person in front of you is about to launch some attack.

Feet and toes

Some philosophers believe moving your feet helps you use your brain. Followers of Aristotle (384–322 BC) were known as *peripatetics* because they walked while they pondered their deep thoughts. Every mile meant a new insight.

A quarter of all human bones are in the feet, and the position of the feet gives much away, especially indicating whether you do or do not have rapport with the other person. Some experts call this 'toeing in' (Figure 5.7, overleaf) as opposed to 'toeing out'.

One canny study even found that members of a jury may unconsciously point their feet away from lawyers with whom they disagree (Figure 5.8, overleaf).

Figure 5.7 Toe in

Figure 5.8 Toe out

'Puffing up'

When toads want to impress other toads, they puff themselves up.
Humans do much the same. We exaggerate our chest and shoulder
size, which is why military uniforms and business suits often are cut
so as to swell our profiles. Some species, like cats, dogs and lions,

puff up their hair to intimidate others. King Kong went further in the best gorilla tradition by thumping his chest. We go to a good hairdresser instead to make our hair look good, which gives the impression that we are in control.

Exercise 5.1: Self-observation

Think of the last time you went to a meeting where you had to impress someone.

- How did you dress?
- Did you behave like a toad?

Head and shoulders

We nod, shake our heads, tilt them up and down. The meaning of some of these movements is obvious, but things are not always that clear when it comes to head tilting.

The head tilt

If we tilt our heads when talking to someone, we are probably unconsciously trying to create rapport. But this is one of those non-verbal behaviours which carries a different meaning when women do it and when men do it. Women who tilt their heads, as Princess Diana often did, tend to appear coy and submissive. There is probably a book to be written on whether Diana tilted her head less as she became less inclined to obey the rules of being a royal.

Figure 5.9 The male head tilt

Men tend to tilt their heads back rather than to the side, and this conveys a very different message from the female head tilt. The male head tilt betrays the fact that someone feels superior, and not remotely submissive (Figure 5.9, page 69). A number of politicians have used this gesture in public speeches, including Al Gore, the Italian Fascist dictator Benito Mussolini and the American president Franklin D. Roosevelt. For all their political differences, when these men tilted their heads back they were showing contempt and scorn. Sometimes, scornful men also lift one eyebrow higher than the other, narrow their eyes, and raise their lower lip.

Hand behind the head or rubbing the back of the neck

When athletes get angry, according to a 1971 study, they often put their hands behind their heads. I have often seen footballers do this – and the gesture starts when we are children. Children often do it when their parents tell them off.

The FBI, which teaches its agents to observe the minutiae of body language, sees this gesture as a useful give-away in interviews. Joe Navarro (2003), one of their experts on non-verbal communication, notes:

> During interviews, I have observed people touching the back of the neck immediately after being told that they are suspect, and then followed up each time the investigators were accurate in describing something only the suspect knew about. I have also noted the speed at which the arm races to the back of the neck and head as being significant, and the amount of

Figure 5.10 Rubbing the back of the neck

force applied once the hand reached the head or back of the neck [Figure 5.10].

Navarro also believes it is useful to look for

the angle of the head and neck as the hand strokes the back of the head or neck. The greater the angle away from the vertical, the more troublesome the issue for the person. I saw a man literally bend forward to the point where he lifted himself off the chair as he brought his hand to the back of the neck and then bent forward as he was being confronted.

The hand or hands behind the head reveal uncertainty, conflict, frustration, anger or dislike. To try to hide such feelings, people sometimes start to massage their necks for comfort.

Desmond Morris argued that when the hand swings up abruptly and clamps itself hard on to the nape of the neck, it is a sign of 'suddenly aroused, but otherwise unexpressed anger'.

Shrugging the shoulders

We shrug our shoulders to suggest we're not too sure of what we're saying (Figure 5.11). This is a non-verbal cue that can modify – and contradict – the meaning of our spoken words.

Figure 5.11 The shoulder shrug

On 11 July 1996, while orbiting in the Russian space station *Mir*, US astronaut Shannon Lucid *shrugged her shoulders, tilted her head*, and gestured with her *palm up* as she answered questions about her six-week delay in returning to Earth. 'You know,' she told NBC's *Today Show*, 'that's life.'

Like our shoulders, our lips can convey many messages.

Lips

The incensed gorilla clenches its lips. In the Highlands of Papua New Guinea, when men were asked to show what they would do when angry and about to attack, psychologist Paul Ekman found 'they pressed their lips together.'

The executive often does the same in the corporate jungle. When your boss is furious, she is apt to clench her lips. A small droop at the corner of the mouth – through the unconscious contraction of a muscle called the *depressor anguli oris* – is often the first sign of grief or disappointment. The compression of the lips is also known as 'the tense mouth look' (Figure 5.12).

Figure 5.12   Clenched lips

As a rule, the more open the mouth, the more relaxed you are. A yawn is the prime example because it shows very openly how bored you are (Figure 5.13). The stifled yawn, where you keep your mouth closed while forcing air through your clenched lips, is a different matter.

Figure 5.13   Yawning

Showing the tongue

Sticking the tongue out is a big gesture of disdain, but very often people just dart their tongues a few millimetres out of their mouths. This tongue-show suggests dislike or disagreement with something that has just been said. Take it as a warning sign. That holds good for gorillas, too. A gorilla pushed from its favourite branch will let its tongue protrude in 'displeasure'.

The tongue-show can be discreet. On my favourite observation ground, the tube, I watched a couple in their thirties. She clenched her lips, chewed them and her tongue protruded in a small tongue-show, but her partner did not notice any of these movements; he was sitting turned slightly away from her, looking at his shopping in the carrier bag at his feet. Suddenly something funny occurred to him and he did the quite unexpected, bumping her with his shoulders and then turning to her. As he caught sight of her tense face he realized something was wrong, but he didn't say anything: he just bumped her again playfully. She suddenly smiled and they became like little kids on dodgems bumping their shoulders against each other. It transformed her mood; a few seconds later her head was on his shoulder. The anxieties that had made her show her tongue had quite disappeared.

Licking the lips is an attempt to comfort ourselves – one of many self-touch movements.

Self-touch

In our stressed society, we often hug, caress, touch our wrists with our hands, pick at ourselves and scratch. Women often fiddle with their arms and inspect their hair for split ends. It would be interesting to know whether there are more self-touches now than in the past. Again, we inherited this way of defusing stress from our ape ancestors. The great student of apes, Jane van Lawick-Goodall noted: 'The more intense the anxiety or conflict situation, the more vigorous the scratching becomes. It typically occurred when the chimpanzees were worried or frightened by my presence or that of a high-ranking chimpanzee' (van Lawick-Goodall 1974: 329).

Motherless rhesus monkeys touch themselves very intensely. They *suck their thumbs or toes, clasp themselves* and engage in *head-banging*. Like psychiatric patients, who often regress in similar ways, the orphaned monkeys feel abandoned and are desperately trying to comfort themselves. Children under stress, like children in Romanian orphanages, often do that. These children also often rock themselves for comfort, a movement that Orthodox Jews adopt when they pray. The more they rock, the more fervent their prayers.

I find it comforting that our most powerful politicians can act just like monkeys. It will be remembered Tony Blair stroked his stomach while Gordon Brown was speaking at a Labour Party conference.

Usually, if you're trying to establish credibility and cool, it looks a lot better if you don't touch yourself.

All these details are instructive, because you don't have to be a slave to your body-language habits. So, in Exercise 5.2, I offer a suggestion to help you change those habits. Partly this is for fun, but partly it is because we all tend to get stuck in a rut. Remove yourself from your rut by following the ideas below.

Exercise 5.2: Self-observation

Write down your most familiar gestures, when you are happy and when you are annoyed.

Think of alternatives – even if they seem ridiculous. For example, next time you are annoyed, instead of tapping your fingers on the coffee table, stand on the coffee table and yawn.

The point of this exercise is to remind you that you don't have to be a slave to the habits of your body language.

Accessories and status symbols

Mobiles

Compare the mobile phone with the worry beads used in some cultures (for example, in Greece). Men fidget with their worry beads to reduce anxiety – and perhaps even to get into a meditative mood. Women fidget with their hair and their jewellery. (See Figure 5.14.)

Figure 5.14   Fidgeting with jewellery

Few of us in the West have worry beads but technology has provided us with an accessory that is even better for expressing anxiety – the mobile phone. The avid interpreter of body language could do worse than look at the poses people adopt in relationship to their mobiles. This has become an interesting area of research, as mobile-phone companies are very rich and desperate to know everything about how people use their mobiles.

Mobiles allow us to express our anxieties. People often caress their mobiles with their fingers as if they're rubbing Aladdin's lamp. If you can intone the right spell, maybe your messages will be magic for you.

Some killjoys – well, killjoys if you are wedded to your mobile phone – fret that now everyone in the West has a mobile glued to their ear, body language may change drastically. As we become ever more absorbed in calling and texting rather than speaking face to face, will we forget to nod and smile at the right moment? The findings are reassuring. Some of us still use body language while we are on the phone, even if nobody is looking at us. A study showed that about 20 per cent of people who talk on mobiles still gesture, smile and nod as though someone else were there to listen and watch.

The research has also established that people tend to adopt two different poses when speaking. One has been called the 'speakeasy' pose. Speakeasies assume an open stance, are happy to be on the phone and let other people see what they are doing. The mobile phone becomes part of their personal display, like an expensive hairdo. They exude confidence, even brio. By contrast some people adopt a more withdrawn 'spacemaker' pose. Spacemakers (who

Figure 5.15 Personal space: the 'Spacemaker'

may have profound psychological issues) create a personal space in which to speak on the mobile. They almost hide the mobile; arms are huddled around the body. When they are sitting, Spacemakers sometimes lift their feet off the ground. These are all signs that they close the world out to focus exclusively on their call. The woman in Figure 5.15 is a good example of a Spacemaker. She is waiting for a tube train. Her head is slightly tilted as she looks down. Her handbag is placed as a defensive shield and helps her create a private space in which she can study her messages in peace.

The interesting psychological question is whether these different poses go with different kinds of personality. I am sure some enterprising social scientist has already offered to investigate, as long as Orange or TalkTalk send a suitably large cheque!

Speakeasies seem to outnumber Spacemakers, though that is only my impression. It certainly seems true that we have fewer and fewer inhibitions about talking animatedly into our mobile phones, so everyone can see whether we are happy or sad. Maybe mobile phones are making the once uptight British less inhibited.

Cars and the gym

Cars are a major status symbol in our society. In most couples, the person who drives most of the time will be the dominant one or the one who can't bear not to be in charge. However, if the driver taps the wheel all the time, this suggests he or she does not feel entirely relaxed.

The gym has become a place where we don't just train but where we show off. The major narcissist will be always checking on himself or herself in the mirror.

Supermarket watch

If you want to become an expert on body language, walk around your local supermarket and watch for the following interactions between couples:

- Who controls the trolley?
- When a couple decide to buy something, do they check with each other?

- When a couple get to the check-out and they realize they have forgotten something, who goes to get it?

You can deduce a great deal from this. The one who stays by the check-out is almost certainly the dominant partner in that relationship in public, because he or she has effectively sent the other one out to fetch and carry. That does not necessarily mean they will be dominant in more intimate situations, but it is very possible.

And finally ...

Finally, a slightly cynical version of some aspects of body language.

What does it mean when a man holds a woman's face *while* kissing?
Please believe me, I'm very serious about kissing you, so shall we tumble into bed?

What message do you send to a man when you tug at your rings?
I'll leave my husband if you'll leave your wife, but before that, Charlie, you're not getting more than a peck on the cheek.

What does it mean when a man puts his thumbs in his trouser pockets while talking to a woman?
Have I got news for you? Or at least, that's what he wants you to believe.

6

The language of the eyes

I crumbled when the boss looked at me and I knew then I couldn't go on lying.

I melted when he looked into my eyes.

These two sentences would fit into any melodramatic novel, but they highlight two things the eyes help us to communicate – that we have every intention of dominating someone (the power gaze) and that we love someone (the love gaze). In this chapter I look at:

- eye contact when we are attracted to someone;
- eye contact when we try to dominate;
- how children learn to make and to respond to eye contact;
- how eye contact helps conversation flow;
- blinking and how we move our eyebrows.

The anatomy of the eye

So they would not miss, infantrymen used to be told, 'Don't shoot till you see the whites of their eyes.' This order would not be much use if you were facing an army of gorillas, however. Human eyes look so white because we lack some pigments found in primate eyes. Most apes have brown or dark 'sclera' or eye surroundings. As a result, one gorilla finds it hard to know exactly where another gorilla is looking.

We also see better just where our fellow humans are looking because there is more contrast between the colour of our eyes and that of our skin. Besides that, we can easily see the outline of someone's eye and its colour because our eyes are more horizontally elongated and disproportionately large given the size of our heads.

Some scientists argue that one reason these traits evolved was to help communication and cooperation. Human infants look at the face and eyes of their mother and father twice as much as baby apes do – and babies learn while they look.

And just as we peer intently at our parents, we peer intently at adults we want to love us. Your eyes, insist psychologists at the Oxford Social Research Centre, 'are probably your most important flirting tool' because they are 'extremely high-powered transmitters of vital social signals'. A recent ad for contact lenses made the point nicely by saying, 'he gazed romantically at her spectacles' – the perfect way to hinder romance! Lovers look into their true love's eyes.

When we are attracted to someone, our eyes change in size and our pupils dilate. It is not conscious but these changes make eye contact 'a powerful and emotionally loaded act of communication', in the words of the Oxford Centre. 'Normally,' they add, 'we restrict it to very brief glances.'

Two people who fancy each other make more eye contact than a 'normal' couple. The would-be lovers also put themselves in positions where they can look at each other more and more directly.

Exercise 6.1: Self-observation – eye contact

Sit opposite your partner.

- Look at each other.
- Now sit side by side.

You will probably make less eye contact in the side-by-side position because you can touch each other without making a point about it, as you do when you hold someone's hand.

Here's looking at you, kid

Good parents lavish eye contact on their babies. The mother tickles, cuddles and feeds her baby – and looks at him or her while she does it. The father does much the same – and looking turns into playing.

These eye games are very old. I'd be willing to bet Stone-Age parents played them. You look at the baby, look away, make a noise like 'coocoocoo', look back. It's fun. Eventually, by the time the baby is about nine months old, these 'sequences' develop into peek-a-boo; this is a vastly important game because it teaches babies that you have to do things in sequence and take turns. You disappear, reappear, disappear again.

Given the importance of eye contact, it is hardly surprising tiny babies can tell when somebody is looking directly at them. Psychologists from London and Padua showed photographs of faces to infants between two and five days old. In one photograph, the eyes were turned to one side (averted gaze). In the other, the eyes looked directly forward (direct gaze). The babies looked longer at photographs of faces in which the eyes looked straight at them.

Figure 6.1 shows the difference between direct gaze and averted gaze.

(a)   (b)

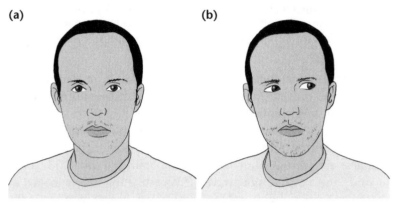

Figure 6.1   Direct gaze and averted gaze

This is reflected in the way the brain processes what we see. By the age of four months, normal babies learn to process information from faces that look directly at them faster than information from faces with averted gaze (Farroni *et al.* 2002). A month later they become even pickier and spend more time looking at faces which have large eyes.

Large eyes will make an impression on you for the rest of your life, especially if you are a man. American men claim they find women with large eyes set widely apart especially attractive. Women speak of how attractive men with large eyes are. (But, oddly, people don't boast of their big soulful eyes in Lonely Heart ads!)

One man who took this science on board was the film director Steven Spielberg. In his film *ET*, he decided it would be a good idea to give the Extra-Terrestrial big eyes so he would look like a baby. *ET* became one of the most commercially successful films in history. I'm not saying it was all down to ET's big eyes – but they probably helped.

Good parenting allows babies to learn some of the rules of eye contact. But when children suffer abuse or have an autistic condition, this very complex system never functions properly – and it has profound effects on their whole behaviour.

Case history

A two-year-old girl diagnosed as autistic tended not to look at her mother, even when the mother put her face directly in front of the child's face. Normal children show toys or objects to their parents, but this girl never did. Her parents said she usually made poor eye contact. One way of getting her attention was to call her by her name, and even that did not work many times; the best way was for them to take their daughter's face in their hands and turn her around so that she had to look at them.

The animal psychologist, Niko Tinbergen (1972), studied autistic children and argued that they were often just scared of too-direct contact – just like birds in some situations.

Brain scientists have studied how babies' brains respond when they see faces that gaze directly at them, and how this differs when the faces are averted. They recorded the brain activity of 33 babies to study the 'positive slow wave' (PSW) while the babies looked at an actress who had been told to assume sad, happy or angry looks (Figure 6.2).

The psychologists found that there were differences in the PSW – but only, they were surprised to discover, when the actress looked angry. They had expected that a smiling face would also trigger a larger positive slow wave, but it didn't. They came up with an interesting explanation. Babies see smiling faces all the time but they do not usually see many angry faces – or at least they don't if their parents care for them properly. So the angry face is a novel face. And what is novel needs immediate attention because it could be threatening, so that triggers a larger positive slow wave.

This was not an isolated result. When damaged children look at faces, the response in their brains is dramatically different to that of normal children. In the 1990s, when the world's media exposed the appalling conditions in Romanian orphanages, one study looked at how the orphans responded to photographs of faces. Seventy-two children aged from seven months to two years eight months looked at photographs in which people looked angry, happy, frightened or

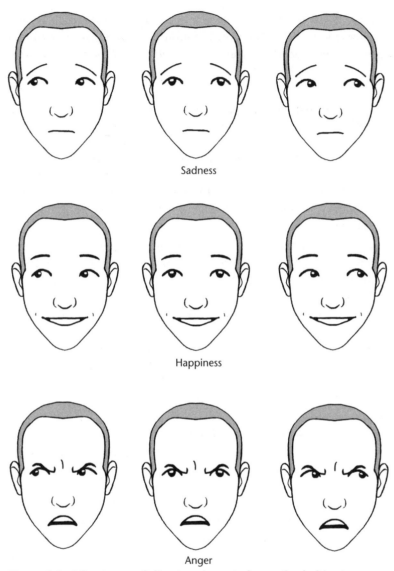

Sadness

Happiness

Anger

Figure 6.2   Nine types of direct and averted gaze for babies to respond to

sad. Their patterns of brain response were very different from those of normal children.

There is one major difference, however, between the eye contact you make with a baby and the eye contact you make with an adult:

you can stare at a baby for a long time without the baby's feeling threatened. And that prompts a question: at what age do children learn that it is rude and/or aggressive to stare? No one seems to have the answer yet.

We think of eye contact as unwavering but, of course, even when we gaze lovingly at someone, we blink. Blinking is one of the basic human reflexes.

Blinking

Normally, we blink about 25 times a minute, though we are not conscious of it, so if we do not blink when we look at someone it is a worrying sign.

Niko Tinbergen said that eye-blinking is a well-known primate movement. 'The moment you have the least little bit of stress, the eyelids blink, bang! bang! bang!'

The eye-blink rate rises from 25 to 50 per minute when someone is interviewed on TV – and far higher if they are on TV to argue that they should be the next President of the United States. In the 1996 presidential debates, candidate Bob Dole averaged 147 blinks a minute – seven times above normal. President Bill Clinton averaged 99 blinks, but that went up to 117 blinks a minute when he was asked tricky questions, like one about the increases in teen drug use during his first term in office.

FBI agent Joe Navarro, whose observations I quoted in the last chapter, finds that a rather higher blinking rate than normal is a good sign of guilt and anxiety. And the FBI has spotted some blinking refinements. Navarro watched when Matt Lauer of NBC's *The Today Show* talked about how Madonna had lied to him about her pregnancy. Navarro argued that when Lauer asked, 'Are you pregnant?' he had missed something the FBI often focuses on – the *eyelid flutter* (see Figure 2.12, p. 29).

The eyelid flutter is different from the eye-blink: under high-speed camera, we can see that the eye does not close completely, and the speed is amazing. Navarro first observed this eyelid behaviour in 1985, and he finds that people who are troubled by a question commonly do this, especially if they are about to lie. 'I tell attorneys to look for the eyelash flutter when they have people on the [witness] stand; it means they really do not like the question at all,' he advises.

The 'listen-and-look' law

Usually when talking, the speaker looks away more than the person who is listening. This is not what you might expect. We are told to look at people when we speak to them, but much research confirms that it gets uncomfortable if you gaze at them too much. So a skilled speaker will spend only about 40 per cent of the time making eye contact and that eye contact will be intermittent. Most episodes of direct gaze will last between one and four seconds – not more.

Eye contact also signals that you have nearly finished. When people are about to end speaking, they will – quite unconsciously – make brief eye contact with their conversation partner. That signals that now it is the other person's turn to speak.

To send the unspoken message that he wants to speak, especially to someone who seems not to want to stop talking, the pattern is different. The listener turns his head away, gestures definitely and breathes in, because he will need plenty of breath to speak.

Tip

Look at the mouth of the person who is listening to you. The mouth should be relaxed and fairly still. It should not be asymmetrical, a position we know reflects discomfort.

One truly off-putting non-verbal signal when you are talking is the stifled yawn, where someone shuts her mouth and puffs out air through her clenched lips. You can see her cheeks balloon slightly when she does this.

When you want to show you are paying concentrated attention to someone who is talking, you need to look at the speaker's face about 60 per cent of the time – more than the more normal 40 per cent.

The basic rules to keep a conversation flowing are:

- glance at the other person's face more when you are listening;
- glance away more when you are speaking;

● make brief eye contact to indicate that in a few seconds the other person should speak.

If someone is distracted he may well smile asymmetrically and turn his head nervously away. A second way of telling whether someone is paying attention to you is to check if he is listening not just to what you are saying but to the rhythm of your conversation. Nodding and smiling are effective ways to encourage someone to talk.

You can control conversations to a surprising extent by such moves. If you nod, if you smile at the person who is talking – especially if you smile when she pauses – she will feel you are a good listener and that you care. This needs to be done subtly or she will feel you are trying to manipulate her.

With eye contact, 'brief' is the key word. Stares that are too long are more threatening than empathic.

Eye contact and power

In the *Dracula* movies of 1931, 1973 and 1979, actors Bela Lugosi, Jack Palance and Frank Langella *widen their eyes* before biting a victim's neck to draw blood. Those who have worked under certain leaders, like General Montgomery, who fought the Battle of El-Alamein, and Manchester United manager, Sir Alex Ferguson, don't compare them to vampires but do talk of the way they look at people piercingly. Strong men and women wilt under the gaze of such supermen. Consciously or unconsciously, they are using what psychologists call *power gaze*.

Sometimes people say that a person who fixes you with this gaze seems to have a third eye in the centre of their forehead – a third eye that stares down at you relentlessly. But we can break the eye's power language into some key elements.

Flashbulb eyes

When we are surprised, two muscles in the eyelids – the *superior* and *inferior tarsals*, to be specific – widen the eye slits to make the eyes look rounder, larger and whiter (Figure 6.3). That happens when we get emotional or feel threatened. The widening allows us to see better out of the corner of our eyes and is controlled by the part of

Figure 6.3   Flashbulb eyes

our nervous system we can crudely call our 'fight-or-flight system'. The fact that physiological signals produce flashbulb eyes makes them hard to fake, so they are very trustworthy signs of *terror* or *rage* which may well precede verbal aggression or physical attack.

Eyebrows can also be revealing.

Eyebrow lowering

Charles Darwin noted that monkeys, especially baboons, when they get angry or excited 'rapidly and incessantly move their eyebrows up and down' (Darwin 1872: 138). And what happens in the jungle also seems to happen in the nursery school. A small child about to hit another child will often first stare at the victim. One scientist found a very specific pattern in children that preceded a fight. He described it as 'what looks like a frown with lowering of the eyebrows and rather little vertical furrowing of the brow ('low frown')' (Nick Blurton Jones 1967: 355). (See Figure 6.4, overleaf)

Sudden lowering of the eyebrows is also a good sign that someone disagrees with you or couldn't care less what you're saying. It's linked to the contempt cues I discussed in Chapter 5 (see p. 70).

Eye movements

It's obvious that where you look can reflect what you are thinking, but some experts also believe that the direction of eye movements is very revealing. They have studied 'conjugate lateral

Figure 6.4 Eyebrow lowering

eye movements', or CLEMs: involuntary eye movements to the right or left that accompany thought. People can be divided into left and right movers because approximately 75 per cent of an individual's conjugate lateral eye movements is in one direction.

One famous study looked at the CLEMs of mathematicians while they were thinking. It found that rightward movement was associated with symbolic thinking, like 'What does A plus B equal?', while leftward movement was associated with visual thinking. Mathematicians whose eyes moved to the left were reckoned by their peers to be more creative.

The most ambitious claims about eye movements have been made by a school of therapy called Neuro-Linguistic Programming (NLP) which started in California.

Frogs into princes

In the 1960s, Richard Bandler and John Grinder, two Californian psychologists who were curious about why some psychotherapists got such good results and others didn't, managed to persuade three famous psychotherapists to let them study how they worked. Their guinea-pigs were impressive. Fritz Perls invented Gestalt therapy, Virginia Satir was a pioneer of family therapy and Milton H. Erickson was a leader in hypnosis-therapy.

Grinder and Bandler analysed the way they spoke, their gestures and their eye movements. They also interviewed some of the people the therapists treated. The results were 'eye-popping'. Patients tended to give clues about their unconscious thinking by the way their eyes moved as well as by changes in posture, gestures and voice tone. Good therapists picked up all this without consciously realizing what they were doing. Bandler and Grinder eventually developed a very precise guide in their book *Frogs into Princes* (1990).

One of their most dramatic claims was that the direction of the eyes reveals whether someone is constructing an image or recalling one. Is it a memory or a fabrication? If someone has to construct an image of an event, clearly that event never happened, so the person must be lying.

Figure 6.5 shows Bandler and Grinder's map of where eyes can move, which is the basis of all their findings.

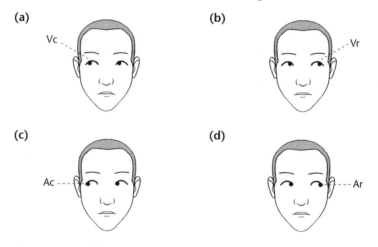

Figure 6.5 Visual accessing clues

Richard Bandler and John Grinder's experiments investigated the direction a 'normally organized' right-handed person looks when asked a question. Based on their results, they claim that:

- *Looking up and to the left* (from the observer's viewpoint) shows this is a *visually constructed (Vc)* image. If you ask someone to imagine a star-spangled pink giraffe – a creature he can't possibly have seen – his eyes will move in this direction while he 'visually constructs' the pink giraffe in his mind.
- *Looking up and to the right* shows this is a *visually remembered (Vr)* image. If you ask someone to remember the colour of her

first car, her eyes will move in this direction while she accesses memories of the battered red car she had when she was 18.

- *Looking to the left* shows this is an *auditory constructed (Ac)* image. If you ask someone to try and create the sound of the highest possible pitch in his head, his eyes will move in this direction while he thinks about the question and tries to construct a sound that he has never heard.

- *Looking to the right* shows this is an *auditory remembered (Ar)* image. If you ask someone to remember what her mother's voice sounds like, this would be the direction her eyes would move in while she tries to hear what she remembers as her mother's voice.

- People who are left-handed will have the opposite meanings for their eye directions.

Neuro-Linguistic Programming (NLP) claims that these findings can be used to detect lies. For example, your friend's daughter asks you for a chocolate biscuit and you say, 'Well, what did your mother say about eating chocolate?' If, when she replies, your friend's daughter looks to the left, this would suggest she is making up the answer. Her eyes are showing her a 'constructed' image or voice. But if she looks to the right, it would indicate a 'remembered' voice or image of something that had happened, so she is telling the truth.

The magician David Blaine has taken an interest in the claims of NLP. But, Blaine suggests, working out whether someone is lying or not from the position of their eyes is not exactly simple; he makes fun of some detectives on TV where the mega-brained sleuth declares, 'The suspect looked down and to the left. Guilty as hell.' Blaine accepts that many critics believe the above is 'a bunch of bull'. But, he adds, 'In my own experiments I have found these techniques to be more true than not.'

The future of eye contact

The science of gaze and eye contact is still an imperfect one. But in the near future we may be able to pinpoint where people are looking and for how long. All we must do is learn the lessons air-force pilots learn. In the cockpit they look at head-up displays as they fly at twice the speed of sound, and the display feeds them a stream of information about targets, where targets are moving and much else besides. They are masters of all they survey.

In the future, spectacles will have head-up displays built into their lenses. So as you walk down the street – at far less than the speed of sound – your high-tech specs will whisper in your ear, 'Man 150 degrees east, looking straight at your breasts for three seconds.'

'Magnify,' you will whisper to your specs. And then you'll make some very hot-cognition instant decisions. Is he good-looking? Is the right response 'flee' or 'flirt'? If he's really attractive, start flirting. At least you will be able to say to him, with absolute conviction, 'I saw you looking at me.'

Will this ever happen? I think it will – partly because something like it is already happening on the High Street. Supermarket chains employ experts who wear specially engineered glasses which allow them to wander round a shop and record how their staff behave with customers. The glasses have a micro camera which transmits to a recorder nearby. The staff, of course, have no idea they are being observed. But the supermarket bosses see all.

It is now time to find out whether the poet was right when he said the eyes are the windows to the soul.

7

The language of the face

'Hell is other people,' said the French philosopher Jean-Paul Sartre. I don't think he got it quite right. It would be more accurate to say: 'Hell is other people who know what you're thinking.' And there is no better way to know what someone is thinking than to look at their face. Every muscle gives you a clue, and these clues work in most cultures – from New York to New Guinea.

Psychologists have found that in every society people find it easy to spot six basic emotional expressions (see Figure 2.2, p. 20):

- happiness
- sadness
- fear
- disgust
- surprise
- anger.

We are astonishingly good at seeing if someone is happy. Only a few people with serious brain damage cannot manage this. We tend to be 80 per cent accurate on the other five emotional expressions. And they can be very subtle expressions. But what we can't be as accurate about is whether someone who looks sad is faking it.

In this chapter I look at:

- how psychologists study facial expressions and how to recognize what they signal;
- how to tell the difference between sincere and insincere smiles, and the meaning of the bared teeth smile;
- movements of the head and face;
- ears and teeth: yes, your teeth can give away that you are a serial killer (more seriously, people reveal quite a lot if they grind their teeth – an indicator of anxiety);

- some fascinating new research on what parts of the brain have to be working well if we are to understand what people feel from the look on their faces.

Exercise 7.1: Self-observation

Look at the face of someone sitting opposite you. See how many different expressions and movements you can spot in five minutes. Even when we sleep our eyes and face move. We can see someone's face frown, relax, pucker, freeze – and smile.

Baby looks

There's nothing as sweet, or as silly, as the mum and dad cooing over the cot and bursting with pride as they say, 'Little Harriet just smiled. Didn't you see her sweet smile?' Babies have been seen to smile when they are just a few hours old, but sceptics tend to argue that this isn't because the baby is overjoyed to have been born to the Jones family in Streatham – it's because she's got wind.

Parents quickly discover that one of the most effective ways to get a smile or a laugh is by tickling. A psychologist called William Preyer reported in 1909 that he could get an eight-week-old baby to smile and laugh by tickling him gently.

You bond with the baby you smile with. Then you start having fun together. The English psychologist C. W. Valentine (1970) noted that one of his sons first laughed at 29 days of age. When that child was five months old, he smiled and whooped cries of joy when he banged the family piano 49 times. Valentine didn't record his own feelings but it's safe to bet that he was smiling at his musical child.

As we grow older we know that – like Richard III – we can smile and 'murder whilst I smile'. Starting from the age of 36 to 48 months, toddlers can smile when they don't mean it. And, as children we learn very fast that smiling can pay.

In my research for my PhD, I found that three-year-old boys and girls who had just done something bad would stop the moment they had smacked another child, giggle winsomely and say 'I am so naughty.' Quite often, their parents and nursery school teachers would smile – and not tell them off very much.

Smile and the world smiles with you

We trust smiling individuals more than people who don't smile (Figure 7.1). Waitresses who smile more get more tips – and political candidates who smile more get more votes. In 50 randomly collected media photographs of George W. Bush and Al Gore taken during the 2000 US election, Bush showed significantly more genuine smiles than the lugubrious Gore. A Gallup Poll before election day showed Bush was rated more trustworthy than Gore. The world has paid the price, we could argue.

Figure 7.1   The trustworthy smile

Smile and the world doesn't just smile with you – it votes for you and hands you cash. Few beggars have taken this on board, however. I make a habit of always giving them some change, because any of us could land on the street, but body-language-challenged street people inevitably only smile after they've got the coin.

So our dilemma is stark. How can we tell the smile being smiled at us is genuine and not a dastardly attempt to con us?

The history of smile research is interesting. About 150 years ago, a French doctor called Guillaume Duchenne started to study smiles. Strangely, he taught a French psychiatrist called Jean Martin Charcot, who taught Freud – who wrote a book on jokes.

Some of the most interesting modern work on genuine and fake smiles has come from an American psychologist, Paul Ekman, who has spent much of his career mapping all the expressions the human face can assume – and working out what you can tell from them.

Exercise 7.2: Self-observation

Try going to work one day smiling. Try going to work not smiling.
    Do people respond to you differently?
    Does anyone ask why you keep smiling all day?

The facial action coding system

Ekman and his colleague Wallace Friesen (1982) produced an atlas of the face that made it possible to break down any facial movement into the smallest 'action units', or AUs, as they called them. Each of these is based on which muscles move.

They could not find anyone else committed enough to spend days producing sad, happy, hurt, scared or disgusted looks, so they had to use themselves as subjects. It was a labour of love. Thanks to their work, we now know which muscles contract to produce any

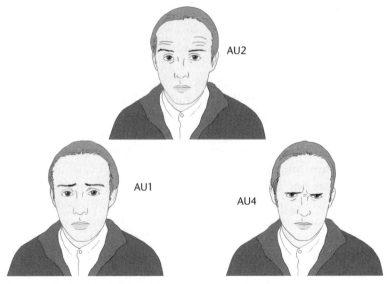

Figure 7.2   Facial action coding

one of the thousands of expressions that flit and fleet across our faces.

They called their way of measuring and decoding expression the Facial Action Coding System (FACS). Figure 7.2 is an example which shows how meticulously detailed their work was.

There are three FACS action units in the brow area. AU 1 (action of the inner *frontalis*) raises the inner corners of the eyebrows, forming wrinkles in the medial part of the brow. AU 2 (action of the outer *frontalis*) raises the outer portion of the eyebrows, forming wrinkles in the lateral part of the brow. AU 4 (action of the *procerus*, *corrugators* and *depressor supercilii*) pulls the eyebrows down and together, forming vertical wrinkles between them and horizontal wrinkles near the *nasion*. The combinations of AUs show how these AUs can act together to form composites of the appearances each produces separately.

When they completed their atlas, Ekman and Friesen were startled by their findings. In the nineteenth century, Duchenne had written about the importance of one facial muscle, the *zygomatic major*, but he had never pushed his research to a final conclusion. Ekman and Friesen did. They found that the ZM, as I'm going to call it, is a real truth-teller because it is never involved in a negative emotional expression. Other muscles are more fickle. The wonderfully named *corrugator*, for example, can be used to convey different emotional messages – happiness, sadness and even disgust.

Not so with the ZM.

A smile in which the lip corners are pulled upward and sideways can be produced by a number of muscles, including the action of the *zygomatic major*, *zygomatic minor*, *buccinator*, *risorius* and *caninus* muscles. But the key question to ask as you look at someone who is smiling at you is this: are they using their zygomatic major?

If they are, they mean it.

If they are not, they are almost certainly being less than sincere.

Exercise 7.3: Self-observation

Look in the mirror. Smile. Learn to spot your own ZM.

Tell your best friend a funny story and watch his face. Does his ZM move?

Tell him a bad joke – and see what happens.

In the 150 years of smile research, however, no one has asked two key questions. First, do people with Machiavellian personalities smile using their zygomatic major muscle? Second, we have seen that babies start to smile when they are about two months old, but at what age do babies start to use their ZM?

When subjects used the ZM, Ekman and Friesen (1982) found, they said they felt happy. There was no such link between other muscles used to produce a smile and the way subjects said they felt. The more active the ZM muscle, the truer the smile.

Checking alternative possibilities, the psychologists also studied what happened when smiles were less spontaneous. They got 36 boys and girls to listen to jokes, and then made the subjects watch expressions of smiling on television. Then they asked them to imitate those TV smiles. When the children listened to jokes, the psychologists argued, the children smiled spontaneously as the jokes had been tested for funniness; when the children were asked to imitate smiles, the psychologists claimed the smiling was less spontaneous, more posed. This difference showed in the muscles they used to produce smiles. When asked to reproduce the smiles they had seen on TV, the boys and girls made less use of the ZM muscle.

Being required to smile deliberately also led to more asymmetrical movements. Why? It owes everything to biology. This is a complex issue but the main argument is clear. Posed smiles, smiles that do not have a real underlying cause, are less intense on the left side of the face. In right-handed people, the left side of the face is controlled by the right side of the brain. To condense 40 years of brain research: the right side of the brain is more emotional and less able to fake than the rational left side of the brain. The left side of the brain controls the right side of the face and can 'tell' it to assume a sincere-seeming smile, but the less devious right side of the brain can't manufacture such a convincing smile on the left-hand side of the face so easily. So the smile on the left-hand side of the face is less intense as a result.

This is not the only clue on which we rely, though. Adults also use the differences between the mouth and the eyes to judge the sincerity of a smile. If the mouth wears a smile while the eyes look down or to the side, for example, we will tend to see the smile as less sincere.

Exercise 7.4: Experiments and games

This is more like charades than serious science. Get a group of friends together. Put on what you think is a happy, sad, angry, disgusted, frightened or surprised look. Don't say a word. This is a test of how well you and your friends can read faces. See how accurately you all guess the following expressions.

- *Happiness*: Should be perfect; 100 per cent of people recognize happy expressions.
- *Sadness*: Usually 80 per cent of those who see a sad face recognize it as such.
- *Anger*: While 80 per cent of people recognize an angry face, most of us are less good at spotting early warning symptoms of anger. If you learn to spot those such as eyebrow lowering, you should be able to avoid fights.
- *Fear*: According to Ekman and Friesen, people recognize fear in photographs 80 per cent of the time.
- *Disgust*: We also recognize a disgusted expression about 80 per cent of the time.
- *Surprise*: Surprise expressions are fleeting, and difficult to detect in real time, according to Ekman and Friesen.

Looks of disgust have been the focus of some very interesting research recently with people who carry the gene for the debilitating disease Huntingdon's Chorea. It has been shown that those with this gene have problems recognizing expressions of disgust, and that this is true both in the West and in China. German scientist Andreas Hennenlotter (2005) has found that these patients have damage to a tiny part of the cortex called the *left dorsal mid-insula*. One real importance of his discovery is that it shows how minutely organized our brains are in terms of recognizing emotional expressions.

And he claims to have found another circuit in the brain that controls the recognition of surprise. Where it is – the *medial temporal lobe* – is important for neuroscience, but for the rest of us what is astonishing is that one millimetre of our cortex must function well for us to spot when someone is surprised.

Altruism

I want to end this chapter by looking at a personality trait you would not think could be spotted through body language.

Four Canadian psychologists claim people can identify who is more altruistic just by watching them. They asked people to read an extract from *Little Red Riding Hood* for one minute, while others watched. The watchers, without knowing it, focused on four aspects of body language that are under involuntary control. These were:

1 the extent of the smile;
2 concern furrows (when your forehead wrinkles);
3 the duration of the smile;
4 smile symmetry.

We cannot control any of these, though a few individuals can manipulate their facial muscles to produce a concern furrow.

The Canadians also looked at non-verbal clues that an individual can control but that are hard to fake. The first of these, you may recall, gave Joe Navarro the idea that Madonna was lying on *The Today Show*. The non-verbal clues were:

1 blinking and eyebrow raises;
2 head nods;
3 open smiles.

They found that the self-declared altruists produced significantly more concern furrows, more head nods, shorter smiles and more symmetrical smiles than non-altruists, all signs that are hard to fake because they are linked to spontaneous emotional expression. And one sign is really not what you would anticipate – the length of the smile. Heartfelt smiles last fleeting instants while a phoney smile stays pasted on the face. As for the altruists' smiles being more symmetrical than those of the non-altruists, the reason probably was that there was less conflict between the rational left side of their brains and the more emotional and more truthful right side.

I have dwelt at some length on this research because it is a powerful example of the way in which people can look at someone's face and work out quite complex aspects of their personality.

8

Body language at work

Elizabeth I of England became queen in 1558. By the time of her death in 1603 she had seen off the King of Spain, the Spanish Armada and a great many would-be husbands. She succeeded in being adored and admired by her subjects, even though she was, in effect, a woman boss at a time when woman bosses were unknown.

By contrast, 300 years later Queen Victoria behaved in ways that made her subjects think she was a poor monarch. She became deeply depressed after her beloved husband Albert died in 1859. After she was bereaved, she was hardly ever seen in public. Pictures of her show a grieving woman who radiates no majesty and little self-confidence. Her favourite prime minister, Disraeli, finally managed to persuade her to show herself more to her subjects. Gradually that changed the public mood in her favour.

What was the difference between the two queens? One was that Elizabeth was a mistress of using body language and was very self-aware, as she made obvious in a famous speech she gave at Tilbury.

> I know I have the body but of a weak and feeble woman; but I have the heart and stomach of a king, and of a king of England too, and think foul scorn that Parma or Spain, or any prince of Europe, should dare to invade the borders of my realm; to which rather than any dishonour shall grow by me, I myself will take up arms, I myself will be your general, judge, and rewarder of every one of your virtues in the field.

Elizabeth spoke as she sat on her horse, the very image of majesty; she looked the absolute opposite of a weak and feeble woman and she was as power-dressed as a sixteenth-century woman could be.

These historical experiences are relevant to the world of work today, where you need to present confident body language. In this chapter I look at research on how to:

- present the best body language in an interview;
- analyse your boss or manager's body language;
- analyse your colleagues' body language;
- handle yourself in meetings;
- project charisma or leadership skills;
- cope if you are being assessed or you are in trouble.

One subject I do not explore, however, is the body language of selling. Many early texts on body language were obsessed with this and gave endless tips on how to establish rapport when you were flogging encyclopedias or vacuum cleaners door to door. I work from home a good deal, and over the last 25 years I have never been visited by anyone offering me an encyclopedia which will change my life. Selling is a very different game now. The salesman knocking on your door is now the person who rings up to peddle all manner of goods or the online drone you never have to see.

Top dog

In the wild, animals – especially social animals like dogs and apes – manage to establish who is the most powerful animal in a group without real violence. If the top dog bit and maimed all the 'inferior' dogs in the pack, the pack would soon become vulnerable. Animals have wisely evolved rituals to show who is top dog without blood being spilt.

Figure 8.1   Wolves displaying dominance and submission

The dominant animal is often bigger and taller. The submissive animal 'knows' that and accepts its place without putting up a real fight. Often the weaker animal offers a vulnerable part of its body to the stronger animal, as in Figure 8.1 (page 101), where a wolf offers its neck to a bigger wolf.

The top dog does not, however, bite the proffered neck because the mere act of having another animal offer up its neck is enough to make clear who is boss. So no one gets injured competing to get the loveliest females or the best cuts of meat.

Human beings are less sane and fight all the time – for serious or utterly trivial reasons. For nearly a century, France, Mexico and the United States warred over a tiny island in the Pacific called Clipperton whose only resource was guano, the droppings of seabirds. In the Middle Ages, there were battles over whether or not men could wear beards.

The Lord of the Bank

In 1975, when I wanted to get an overdraft, I went to see the all-powerful bank manager. He – it was always a man in those days – sat behind his desk in his inner sanctum, a polished office with a huge polished desk. An assistant opened the door and led me in. I did not offer my neck to the bank manager, but I remember always feeling tense and trying to make the best impression.

Thirty years later, I went to review my 'banking requirements' at the West-End office of my bank. My new bank manager emerged from a massive open-plan office. She did even not rate an office of her own. Yes, big news, we have women bank managers – but when she met a client she had to share a desk in a small cubicle. She had no assistant to get a cup of coffee. Her office and her body language reflected the truth that my deskless bank manager does not have anything like the power her predecessors had in 1975.

Derek Spencer, John Temple, Ian Springett and Bob Cumber, nice men who sat behind the magnificent desk in the NatWest branch at Knightsbridge, could decide to lend large sums because the job of the bank manager then was to decide who was a good risk and who wasn't. They were expert at intimidating body language and masters of the fixed stare. Once, I left the manager's office sweating because he complained I was always up to the limit of my overdraft and sometimes over it; I tried hard not to display signs of tense body language as that would have made a bad impression.

Then, only the very biggest decisions were referred to what one of them called 'the gods at Lothbury', where the headquarters of the bank were located. But now the bank manager has much less status. Almost all lending decisions are made centrally by the bank computer. It looks at your history, consults your credit rating and decides yes or no.

The very different work spaces these managers enjoyed high-lights the loss of status. In 1975, the manager had power – and assistants to fetch tea or coffee – as well as an impressive desk; in 2007, he or she has no desk, no assistants and not much power.

Times change. And one change that has affected most of us is that we have much less job security than people had years ago. This means, of course, that we are much more likely to have to seek new jobs.

Body language at interviews

Every year in the United Kingdom millions of people go for job interviews, whether for a supermarket or a management position, body language is crucial.

Much advice suggests you should be quite submissive. Never give the idea that you may be a tough or dominant person. After all, you, the candidate, are the one asking for a job.

Some experts suggest you should shower the interviewer with positive feedback. One gem of advice from self-help websites (for example, <www.nationalbullyinghelpline.co.uk>) is to sit up and lean slightly forward as that will project 'interest and engagement in the interaction. It is also wise to align your body's position to that of the interviewer as that shows admiration and agreement' (Figure 8.2, overleaf). Flattery will get you hired.

Interviewees should also: 'Show your enthusiasm by keeping an interested expression. Nod and make positive gestures in modera-tion but avoid looking like a bobblehead.'

And, a little bizarrely, 'Stand up and smile even if you are on

Figure 8.2 Mirroring posture in an interview

a phone interview. Standing increases your level of alertness and allows you to become more engaged in the conversation.'

Dire don'ts

- Don't rub your neck – which suggests you don't care or have something to hide.
- Don't rub your nose – which is unpleasant and suggests you are lying.
- Don't rub any other part of your anatomy either – which is even worse.
- Don't shake or 'bobble' your legs or knees – which suggests tension; if anyone on the interview panel has been in the police they will suspect you have a criminal past.
- Don't stare blankly at the panel – which suggests that you haven't got a single idea in your head.

The problem with advice that urges you to be submissive is that it ignores the kind of job you are going for. If you hope to become Junior Accounts Clerk no. 77, the advice is probably sound. But if the job involves making decisions and managing other people, a competent interviewing panel may well conclude that, with your pathetically submissive body language, you are not commanding enough.

So work out what the job really demands before you decide what body language messages to send.

Nevertheless, there are three kinds of non-verbal communication that it nearly always pays to show.

1 Give the interviewing panel your total attention using all the skills so far described. This is what the great therapist Carl Rogers offered his clients.
2 Do some mirroring – but not too much.
3 A bit of enthusiasm rarely does any harm. This should be both verbal and non-verbal.

Then, whether you fail or succeed, ask for feedback, which most employers now offer. It may be painful to hear that you spoke hesitantly and looked confused when you were asked tough questions, but feedback will give you vital information about the way others see you – and what you need to change to perform better at your next interview. If you get the job, still ask for feedback. You are going to have to work with these people so you must know how they see you.

Tip

Be consistent in your presentation of yourself. Do not act like a weakling when you give one answer and like a tough nut when you give the next, unless you can explain why you are presenting such different personalities. Good interviewers will pick up contradictions swiftly.

A number of American websites also offer the following suggestion to people being interviewed: limit your application of colognes and perfumes. Invasive aromas can arouse allergies. Being the candidate that gave the interviewer a headache isn't going to work in your favour. (Body language do's and don'ts for interviews, which can be found at <www.CareerBuilder.com>)

Case history: The lying CV

I became very aware of just how damaging contradictions can be in the way you present yourself when I was asked to film candidates for the job of chief executive of a medium-sized company. The recruitment agency wanted to see how potential chief execs might behave if they were being interviewed by the media. The results were instructive.

Two candidates became very nervous. One was a woman who had come in a dramatic orange dress with orange-dyed hair; her appearance disqualified her entirely, I thought. But what I found most interesting was the erratic body language of one male candidate. He would lean back and stare into the distance as if musing deep personal thoughts. Then, suddenly, he would snap to, lean forward, smile intensely at me and become animated and forceful, using his index finger in a classic jab to emphasize points he was making. Finally, all aggression drained, he would lean back in his chair again, ruffle his hands through his hair and avoid eye contact.

Odd, I thought.

Though his CV was excellent and suggested he was well qualified, his body language suggested something different. He was over-anxious and seemed to find it hard to pay attention. His sudden aggressive movements suggested he might well be a bully as a boss. I subsequently learned that that his CV had been misleading and that he had been asked to leave his last job. He had not been frank about that.

In the job

Once you have a job, you need to assess the company you are working for. What is it like? And here the body language both of your boss and of your colleagues may be very revealing. The first vital step is to work out the leadership style of the person you report to.

Daniel Goleman in 'Leadership That Gets Results' (2002) (*Harvard Business Review*) offers a good guide. He describes six leadership styles: Coercive, Authoritative, Affiliative, Democratic, Pacesetting and Coaching.

- The Coercive leader demands immediate obedience and does not tolerate dissent.
- The Authoritative leader tries to inspire people with his vision and radiates self-confidence, but wants things done his way.

- The Affiliative leader builds bonds. She believes harmony will get the best results. Good teamwork makes money.
- The Democratic leader forges consensus by asking people what they think and emphasizes team leadership and collaboration.
- The Pacesetting leader sets a high standard of performance and does not really care about hurting people's feelings very much.
- The Coaching leader likes to act as a headmaster. In the last episode of one series of *The Apprentice*, Sir Alan Sugar joked that he was resigned to having to mentor and headmaster his latest recruit because he would need encouragement and guidance.

Clever leaders use each of these styles at different times though, Goleman argues, leadership should never be Coercive. The best results, in terms of performance and of creating a happy ship, come when bosses can switch easily between the Authoritative, Democratic, Affiliative and Coaching styles.

How do you work out which is true of your boss?

Exercise 8.1: Watching the boss

Observe your manager and score him or her on the following behaviours.

1 Does he let others have their turn to speak?
2 Does she usually keep the door of her office open unless there is a good reason for privacy?
3 Does he bite his nails or scratch other parts of his anatomy?
4 Does she invade personal space? (An extreme example would be sitting on your desk when coming to talk to you; a less extreme example is peering over your shoulder at you while you work.)
5 Does he pace around the open-plan office looking to see what you are doing?
6 Does he or she flirt with employees?
7 When your boss listens, does he lean towards the speaker, rewarding him or her with head nods and making eye contact?
8 Does your boss show signs of chronic impatience?
9 Is your boss good at giving praise? If something has gone badly, does she discuss calmly what has gone wrong?
10 Does your boss share his worries when your team's performance is about to be reviewed by top management?

Yes to Questions 1, 2, 7, 9 and 10 suggests that your boss shows signs
of being a good manager.

Yes to Questions 3, 4, 5, 6 and 8 suggests she or he is very anxious and
tries to deflect that by being aggressive and rude to others.

If your boss scored a no to most of Questions 1, 2, 7, 9 and 10 and
yes to most of Questions 3, 4, 5, 6 and 8, you are not likely to be in a
happy environment.

Bad managers give themselves away not just by their words and
memos but by their body language. They show that they are bored
by picking their fingernails or imaginary spots on their clothes.
Both of these are, according to some occupational psychologists,
variations on the act of jiggling your knees – which is given the
wonderful technical description 'knee bobbling'.

360 degrees of hell

In the past there was very little employees could do if they were
being managed badly. But things have changed, partly because
of a new technique called '360-degree assessment' which requires
managers to be assessed not just by their superiors, but also by their
peers and juniors. The questions ask you to reflect on the body
language of the person you are assessing as well as how competent
they seem to you. This new technique puts great pressure on managers. One chief executive I know was devastated to discover that
his employees thought he was rather vague and lazy. He retired
soon after.

   If you feel especially vicious, you will jot down all the person's
worst and most off-putting actions. Spiteful? Very. And office
tensions can produce such feelings. But the increasing use of the
technique of 360-degree assessment also means that you yourself
are likely to be subject to such an examination. So be careful how
you present yourself to those above – and below – you.

Office spaces

In the office, one key weapon is your work space or desk. Good receptionists, for example, use their desk as a boundary. You will not get past it if they don't want to let you in.

Inside the office, the desk is your own territory. Organizational psychologists have found three basic positions in which people place their desks:

- in the corner, so the person sitting at it is 'enthroned', sees everything and is protected on three sides (Figure 8.3);
- facing the window, so when someone comes in they are greeted by the desk owner's back;
- placed centrally, so that a visitor can stand or sit opposite you at the front but also can come to one side of desk.

The first position gives the desk owner a sense of control as it protects the rear and sides. The second position is the most vulnerable, as the desk owner prefers a nice view of the outside to watching everything taking place in his space. The third position is the compromise, as the desk owner can see what is happening but also grants some room to a visitor.

Research into body language is only just catching up with new work arrangements such as open-plan offices, call centres and

Figure 8.3   Sitting 'enthroned' at a corner desk

working from home, but some of the principles of work body language are very old.

Body language at meetings

The meeting is the bane of corporate life today. Meetings these days have a special lingo where people say things like: 'Can I parachute in on that one?' and 'Please don't be such a silo'. (That's government jargon for 'single interest lobby'; if you are too much of a silo, you don't see the whole picture).

Non-verbal communication is, at least, less quirky than corporate jargon. What is crucial is knowing how to make your points firmly without upsetting people, and posture and timing matter. Do not slouch at meetings: sit up at the table and make notes. Make steady eye contact when others are speaking. And try to sense the mood of the meeting. You can do this by checking how much tense body language is on display. You would be well advised not to start confrontations if you can see many examples of displacement activities, fidgeting or classic signs of tension, such as people sitting with their arms crossed or rubbing their hands on the back of their heads (Figure 8.4).

If you are ambitious, you will want promotion. Obviously, Human Resources will consider your whole work record. But it will also help if you behave like a potential leader without

Figure 8.4   Body language at a meeting

making your managers and colleagues feel you are irritatingly ambitious.

By this point in the book you should have some idea of what you need to project to make people feel that about you.

Exercise 8.2: Self-observation

Write down seven things you can do to convince work colleagues that you would make a good leader.

If there is someone you trust at work – especially someone you trust not to betray your ambitions – discuss these, and in the light of what he or she says, modify your tactics.

Take a deep breath and work out the risks of trying a few of them and seeing how people respond to you.

Women bosses

Surveys by the website Badbossology (<www.Badbossology.com>), which records what makes good and bad bosses, show that men over 45 find it hard to cope with a woman boss because, histori-cally, women were meant to be submissive. Men who now have women bosses sometimes resent having to report to the so-called 'weaker sex'. The reversal of roles can cause problems.

Tip

Try to forget your boss is a woman and treat her as you would a male boss.

But we are in the middle of many social changes, which can cause confusion. An article for *Woman* magazine, for example, recently reported on men who had relationships with powerful career women. Yes, the women were used to lording (or should it be ladying?) it over minions at the office, but the moment they got home, the article said, they wanted to relax. And they relaxed by being submissive to their 'inferior' men – especially in bed. How extraordinary that a leading women's magazine should publish what seemed to be a very sexist piece.

Maximum stress:
the bizarre business of paradoxical intention

It is vital to present good body language during assessments or if you are in trouble. If the boss is criticizing you – or, worse, if you face a disciplinary hearing – you need to appear reasonably confident. That does not mean you must never apologize, but your body language must not suggest you are wracked with anxiety – even though you may well be.

The first obvious tip is to try to relax before the meeting. That's easier said than done, but it may be helpful to ask your partner or your closest friend what tells them you are feeling nervous.

The second trick is surprising. Do not always suppress those tics and twiddles, at least when you are preparing for what is bound to be a tense meeting. Instead, go in for 'paradoxical intention'. That's a concept that needs explanation.

Case history
Consider the following story about a civil servant in an Eastern European country.

When the man retired to his country cottage, he caused a stir in the village. Every morning one of the local boys would call and disappear for a minute or so into the man's cottage. The curious villagers persuaded the boy to reveal what was going on: 'I am paid to knock on his bedroom door and shout a few words and then he shouts a few words.' He finally told them what these words were. He said: 'I shout, "The Secretary of State wishes to see you," and he shouts back "To hell with the Secretary of State."''

The civil servant was finally getting his own back after years of kow-towing to his boss. But the man was also using a variant of a technique called 'paradoxical intention', though he had no idea he was doing that.

A clever psychoanalyst, Viktor Frankl, argued that there was no need to spend months on the couch to cure yourself. If you felt depressed, you should consciously try to make yourself as depressed as possible. If you were anxious you should make yourself as anxious as possible. Frankl claimed that pushing to the limits, paradoxically, made people feel less depressed and less anxious. Frankl incorporated this technique successfully into the therapy he practised.

In terms of body language, his ideas can be applied. The sequence seems simple. First, identify the signs that tell you that you are stressed. Let's assume you know you fidget and sigh when you are anxious and that is precisely what you do, and feel, as you await the dreaded assessment. Now breathe deeply and attempt the paradoxical cure. It is highly practical.

Your problem is that you fidget? You haven't tried fidgeting yet. How long can you fidget?

Let's see. Not very good. You're a midget in the fidget stakes. You have to fidget with your fingers, toes, knees till it's impossible to fidget more.

Repeat the exercise with sighing. Sigh, sigh and keep on sighing. You may discover you can't sigh for much more than five minutes.

What other signs of nervousness do you show? Display them as much as you can.

This technique will not cure the underlying causes of stress but it will help you achieve a measure of control over them. It may also make you laugh!

And laughter is often the best medicine. Very oddly, not much has been written about the body language of laughter. Laughter really shakes the body; it is one of only four actions in which we cease to be in control of our bodies. We don't become helpless when we talk, but when we laugh, sneeze, have an orgasm or are in extreme distress we are out of control.

In 1955, a psychoanalyst reported a case of a six-year-old boy who could not stop laughing. In 1982, the *Lancet* noted, with a mixture of alarm and amusement, that 25 per cent of student nurses admitted to having had an experience of 'giggle incontinence', laughing so much that they wet themselves. More positively, when you laugh you release neuro-chemicals in your brain which promote a sense of euphoria.

So laugh at those aspects of your body language which will suggest to anyone sitting in judgment on you that you might be nervous. Once you have done that, you are likely to face your tense meeting more calmly.

Here are some less unusual tips for preparing for assessments or 'I am in trouble' meetings.

Tips

- Concentrate, so you can be very aware of the body language of those on the other side.
- Do not get into an eye-contact war.
- Do not stare down at papers or your feet, which will suggest you are trying to hide something.

Mastering your own body language is also helpful in dealing with an all-too-common work problem.

Bullying

In America 20 million people report feeling bullied at work, while a British study claims that 81 per cent of workers report having been bullied. In my early twenties I worked for a bully; he never praised good work and always blamed me or my colleagues if something did not go to plan. He made me so anxious that I rejected the offer of a new contract from the company and left.

Bullies are not subtle. They try to get their way by adopting threatening postures, shouting and turning up unexpectedly to see what you are up to. 'Keep everyone on edge' is their management style; they think their being unpredictable will make people work harder. It is actually not the truth.

Some commentators now think political correctness has made us too ready to accuse bullies. Mick Hume in *The Times* argued this in the case of Helen Green. She sued Deutsche Bank because four female colleagues made belittling remarks, would not talk to her and blew raspberries when she was making investment decisions. Ms Green had a nervous breakdown. But Hume said: 'I see no evidence that workplace bullying is getting worse – rather, we are more willing to see ordinary office politics as bullying.'

Hume also marvelled at the fact that even the armed forces now have to worry about bullying. He cited the case of a regimental sergeant-major at Sandhurst who had been suspended for allegedly bullying cadets by shouting obscenities at them – 'Sergeant Swears at Recruits', the horror of it – and stamping on the less-than-shiny boots of one young man. The Ministry of Defence explained bizarrely that the cadet was not wearing his boots at the time.

Hume ignores the fact that bullying can damage people psychologically and, in extreme cases, even drive them to suicide. Four deaths of young recruits at Deepcut army barracks seem to have been caused by the fact that they felt so bullied.

So how can knowledge of body language help deflect bullying?

Exercise 8.3: Self-observation

Are you bullied?

What does being bullied make you feel like?

What kind of body language responses do you then show?

Write down three instances of when you feel you have been bullied.

What did you do in response?

Work expert Robert Mueller (2005) gives advice on how to change from a target into a confident Workplace Warrior. One of the most valuable tools Mueller offers is the Incident Report form. If you feel bullied, you should methodically record any instances of abuse – and not just in case you decide to sue. The process of documenting the abuse will help you understand it, help you spot patterns in the way your managers are behaving, and help you devise methods to combat it.

Sadly, bullying can also occur in more intimate situations, especially in families. The recent shocking revelations of how perhaps 600,000 old people in Britain are abused make that very plain. For more on this, see Susan Elliot-Wright, *Overcoming Emotional Abuse* (2007).

9

The body language
of flirting and fancying

In the 1989 hit film *When Harry Met Sally*, the couple stop at a restaurant on the way to New York. Over hamburgers, they bicker about how men and women see – and make – love. To show how vain men are all too easy to fool, Sally (played by Meg Ryan) gives a virtuoso display of a girl having an orgasm. All a girl has to do is breathe ever more frantically, loll her head back and start screaming 'Yes! Yes! Yes! It's good!' The other diners listen in; one woman says she'll have whatever Meg Ryan is eating. Harry (played by Billy Crystal) gets embarrassed, and not just because his friend is making a spectacle of herself. The deeper reason is that men do not like to be reminded of the fact that women can fake orgasms.

Very wittily, the scene shows that we never know what someone really feels. That is why we are so eager to read the body language of attraction and arousal. Even today, 40 years after the sexually permissive society started to permit, sex is still surrounded by many taboos. And taboos mean anxiety – and anxiety shows in body language.

In this chapter I look at

- flirting and personal space;
- gay flirting;
- differences in the way men and women communicate;
- where men and women look when talking to each other;
- how personality affects sexual interaction.

Exercise 9.1: Signs of love?

How do you know if someone fancies you? Write down at least four key things you think are good clues.

116

If you are in a relationship, what signs do you look for to tell whether your partner is in a romantic mood?

If it's a good relationship, ask your partner: 'Do you recognize those signs as something that you do when you want me to get in a loving mood?'

Michael Argyle, the academic I mentioned in Chapter 1, pioneered studies of how men and women look at each other and look away. This is one of the oldest eye ballets in the world – you look at someone who interests you, but you don't want them to realize you are keen so you look away. Then, out of the corner of your eye, you wait for them to look at you – which will show whether they are interested too.

The way we look at someone else is something of a precision skill. This applies especially when a man and a woman meet for the first time. The situation is tense and risky. Neither knows what the other person thinks, feels or wants.

Usually we tend to be less direct because we worry about being rejected. The Oxford Social Research Centre warns that women should be careful about flaunting their body language, as men are all too ready to mistake friendliness for flirting – and flirting for mad, passionate desire. But that, of course, does not mean that women never initiate flirting.

In *Psychology Today*, Monica Moore (1995) reported what is known as a meta analysis of studies of flirting. Looking at a mass of research, Moore found that women use 52 different non-verbal courtship behaviours. These included glancing, gazing, primping, preening, smiling, lip-licking, pouting, giggling, laughing and nodding. Her research slammed the myth that it is always men who start the dance; often girls take the first step. There were many instances, Moore saw, when a woman looked round a room to spot any likely talent. When her eyes lit on a likely candidate, a girl tended to flash the short darting glance – looking at him, quickly looking away, looking back and then away again. Many women managed this in a shy, sly and indirect way (Figure 9.1, overleaf).

Figure 9.1   Flirting

In today's world, however, where magazines for pre-teen girls often discuss sex, women are frequently more overt. Moore even saw a few women hike their skirts up so that the man they fancied could ogle more of their legs. But when they realized other men were looking at their thighs, these 'come-and-get-me' girls quickly pulled their skirts down again.

Moore found many examples of flirting body language, including:

- the eyebrow flash – an exaggerated raising of the eyebrows of both eyes, followed by a rapid lowering;
- the coy smile – tilting the head down, looking away at an angle;
- turning the head to expose some of the neck.

Many experts see these as signs of female submissiveness, but Moore argues that this is a mistake. These moves are not submissive because their point is 'to orchestrate courtship', and the one who orchestrates moves is not powerless.

Moore is not the only expert to think that we need to be more

modern and not view flirting as a battle of the strong male and the submissive female. Tim Perper (1999) of the University of Philadelphia
argues that men who flirt produce gestures that may look dominant,
such as sticking out their chests and strutting around. But don't let
the bravado fool you. The dominant flirt may also show many submissive gestures, such as bowing his head lower than the woman's.
Women may also yo-yo between the dominant and the submissive,
Perper notes. A woman may drop her head, turn slightly and bare
her neck, but then 'lift her eyes and lean forward with her breasts
held out, and that doesn't look submissive at all', he argues.

The latest research concludes that no one is ever totally dominant in a good flirtation. Instead, there is a subtle, rhythmical and
playful back-and-forth. A couple synchronize. She turns, he turns;
she picks up her drink, he picks up his drink.

Tip

Skilful operators do it gradually. You can show a stranger you're
interested across a crowded room by looking at him or her and
trying to hold the gaze for roughly one second. Much more than one
second tends to be perceived as threatening. If the subject of your
interest keeps eye contact with you for more than one second, he or
she might well be interested too.

What happens next is important. If, after the one second plus,
the subject looks away and does not look back at you in the next
30 seconds, you can assume they have no real interest in you. But if
you catch them looking back to meet your eye a second time, they
probably like you.

Flirting and personal space

When you try to flirt with someone, the distance you keep from
them matters. First, don't get carried away because you feel randy
or romantic. Your potential flirt may feel differently. Look! Notice
how far they stay from you. That reveals much about their feelings
towards you (Figure 9.2, overleaf).

Second, if you haven't established eye contact yet, it is far too
early to even think about flirting.

Figure 9.2   Appraising the potential for flirting

Tip

When you are about two small steps away, you are on the border between the 'social zone' (120–360 cm) and the 'personal zone' (45–120 cm).

If your hoped-for flirt smiles or returns your gaze, you can come closer. The best distance is 'arm's length', or just under a metre. Any closer and you are moving into the 'intimate zone' border reserved for lovers, family and very close friends. This might make your target uncomfortable.

Exercise 9.2: Self-observation

How do you behave when you flirt?

What tells you whether it is serious or not?

Try to remember the first time you flirted.

Look objectively at your flirt's posture. Encouraging signs are if he or she is also leaning forward and has an 'open' posture. Women, experiments show, are more likely to tilt their heads to one side when they are interested.

Another positive sign is mirroring, when the mirror neurons are firing and your partner gets into a posture similar to yours. Mirror-image postures – where one person's left side 'matches' the other person's right side – are the strongest sign of rapport. It is usually best if people are not consciously aware of someone deliberately 'echoing' their postures, though they will still view a person who does this quite favourably. But don't go too far, especially these days, when so many people now are savvy about body language.

Barrier signals

If the person you are trying to flirt with is not keen, they may respond with obvious barrier signals such as turning away or crossing their arms. There is also a very subtle 'keep out' sign to watch for. The not-keen may rub his neck and point his elbow upwards at you. Back off if that is the reaction.

If only the person's head is turned towards you while the rest of the body is oriented in another direction, this too is a negative sign. A woman also can use a handbag as a barrier (Figure 9.3).

Figure 9.3   Personal barrier signals

Moore also noted the ways women slow down a flirtation or stop the whole tango. To slow down, a woman will tend to orient her body away slightly, cross her arms across her chest, or refuse eye contact. To finito the tango in its tracks so there would be no chance of it ever resuming, Moore saw, women might frown, sneer, shake their heads from side to side, put their hands in their pockets, stare over the bloke's head, flirt with other men or just yawn.

Moore also observed situations in which men showed the sensitivity of an armadillo. Among desperate don't-bore-me manoeuvres women had to resort to, some held a strand of hair up to their eyes – message: I'd rather examine my split ends than spend another moment with you. Or, the ultimate turn-off, some women picked their teeth.

The best flirting distance

The rules for the best distance for flirting differ depending on whether you are face to face or side by side. When side by side with someone, eye contact is inevitably less direct and less intense. Each of you has to turn your head to look directly at the other person. To compensate – and this is unconscious – you nudge and huddle a bit closer than 'arm's length'.

Gay flirting

Gay flirting has been studied less than heterosexual flirting but some research hints at interesting differences. Marny Hall (1999), a San Francisco psychologist, remembers that, back in the 1950s, gay women stuck to inflexible gender roles. Butch women did the male stuff. They held their bodies tight, lit cigarettes with a dominating flourish, bought drinks, opened doors and swaggered. On the other hand, 'femmes' would wiggle their hips and use indirect feminine wiles.

In the 1960s, that changed and lesbians shied away from artifice. In the 1990s, however, the butch–femme distinction came back. But with one big difference. Today's lesbians have a sense of irony and wit about the whole charade and the butch–femme distinction is less polarized. 'The gender roles are more scrambled, with "dominant femmes" and "soft butches",' Hall observes.

Irony is interesting here. You don't find it that often in straight flirting, because even if women are a little bit more likely to take the initiative than in the past, sex roles are still set in the mould.

Male homosexuals also flirt in ways that might surprise heteros. Social psychologist Timothy Perper observed two gay men locked in a stalemate of sustained eye contact for 45 minutes. Only then did one of them make the next move. That was a slow couple: Perper has also seen two gay men fast forward in two minutes through the whole flirting ritual of 'gaze, approach, talk, turn, touch, synchronize'. And so to bed, in a way Samuel Pepys would have approved of. Such dazzling speed is unusual in heterosexual relationships. Even the great lover Casanova usually took an hour – and quite often a day – to consummate his liaisons.

Gay men who want to commit can also now take dating courses, which began at the Harvey Milk Institute in San Francisco in the 1990s. One topic is the repertoire of gestures straight women use when they are seeking partners. Gay men are encouraged to learn how straight women do it.

Finally, I must record a confusing flirting incident on a train. A gay lawyer, Anthony, sat opposite a gay prison officer, Tracey. They hadn't met before but, after half an hour, they were flirting enthusiastically and arranging to go out together, so that he could pick up men and she could pick up women. Their flirting signals were similar to those you might see a heterosexual pair exhibiting, expect that Tracey and Anthony occasionally slapped each other's hands in 'high fives', while shouting: 'Gay pride!'

When men and women talk

Deborah Tannen is one of the world's experts on the differences in the ways men and women listen and talk. I interviewed her for *New Scientist* in 1992 after she had published a book called *You Just Don't Understand* (1992).

Tannen told me women frequently complain that their husbands or partners don't talk to them. She referred me to her book *Divorce Talk*, which claims that most women – but only a few men – give lack of communication as the reason for their divorce. As half the marriages in the USA fail, Tannen added, 'This amounts to a virtual epidemic of failed conversation.'

Figure 9.4   The linguistic battle of the sexes

A familiar cartoon summed it up for her. Husband is sitting at the breakfast table reading the morning paper which is in front of his face, while his wife glares at the newsprint (Figure 9.4). He wants to read; she wants to talk. It's the linguistic battle of the sexes, according to Tannen. And one that causes much suffering – avoidable suffering, in her opinion.

Tannen conceded that when women accuse men of not listening and men protest, 'I *am* listening,' the men are often right. But their body language does not make the women think that the men are paying attention.

'Something has gone wrong in the mechanics of male–female conversation,' Tannen said. The problem starts, according to Tannen, as soon as a man and a woman position themselves to talk. When she studied videotapes made by psychologist Bruce Dorval of children and adults talking to their best friends of the same sex,

> I found that at every age, the girls and women faced each other directly, their eyes anchored on each other's faces. At every age, the boys and men sat at angles to each other and looked elsewhere in the room, periodically glancing at each other.

But when men face away from them, women interpret this as indifference: the creeps aren't listening. And that leads to bitterness and hostility.

The reasons women think men don't listen can be even simpler. Lynette Hirschman, a linguist, found women made more listener-noises, such as 'mhm', 'uhuh' and 'yeah', to show that they were in tune with their partner. Men make far fewer such noises and women interpret the almost-silence to mean men couldn't care less what they're saying. Men, on the other hand, interpret these small burbles of noise as meaning 'Just get on with it, darling' or 'Don't make a fuss' – signs of impatience.

Let's be honest, gentlemen (and I write here as a man, of course). We men usually hate it when a girl says, 'We need to talk.' We know she will want to talk about the relationship and not Real Madrid; we know we shouldn't sigh inwardly but hey, chaps, football is more interesting than feelings ... I jest.

A young woman told Tannen that whenever she said she wanted to talk, her boyfriend would lie down on the floor, close his eyes and put his arm over his face. She took this to mean that he'd rather take a nap than listen to her. But her boyfriend insisted that he was making the 'supreme sacrifice of listening' with his ears fully attuned. He shut his eyes so he could concentrate on her every syllable. She didn't believe a word he said but, after listening to Tannen, she found the courage to explain how frustrated he was making her – and why.

The next time she made it obvious she wanted to talk, her boyfriend lay down as usual and covered his eyes. She muzzled her usual irritation, made sure he really was listening and was amazed by what followed.

The boyfriend sat up and looked at her. Thrilled, she asked why. He said, 'You like me to look at you when we talk, so I'll try to do it.' Problem solved. But it took courage and compromise from both of them.

Where men and women look

Men are all too apt to stare at a woman's breasts rather than her face. But women tend to look desirable men up and down from head to toe!

Exercise 9.3: Self-observation – where do you think you look?

If you have a video camera, video yourself looking at two people of the opposite sex, one person you know and one person you hardly know, for five minutes. Let them do the same.

Play the video back, and you should be able to spot roughly where you and they are looking.

Personality

I have suggested that personality affects body language. It also affects the way, and the speed, at which people interact sexually – and how body language reveals that. For example, Eysenck's theory of personality has implications for sex (1973). He quipped that 'when all is said and done, more is said than done'. Extroverts are more impatient, get bored more easily and become sexually aroused faster. As a result, men who are extroverts will want to hurry towards sex – and probably through sex. Introverts, on the other hand, will proceed more slowly, which would make them better lovers if it were not for the fact that they also get more anxious.

Figure 9.5   Couples and personal space: equal interest

Figure 9.6   Couples and personal space: unequal interest

Problems are likely when two lovers, or would-be lovers, have different personality styles. They may find it hard to adapt to each other's rhythms. So the classic mismatch is the 'get your clothes off in a hurry' extrovert and the 'I get so anxious, please don't rush' introvert. And the risk is that the one in a hurry is so eager he doesn't notice the signs that say 'Please slow down.'

For men especially, it's wise to analyse your own past – and face up to the question of whether you get too keen too fast and whether that betrays itself in your body language.

The couple in Figure 9.5 are mirroring, bent towards each other and creating a shared personal space. The couple in Figure 9.6 are very different. He is very keen but she is staring at her feet, which are pointed towards the door, through which she'd like to escape.

Men need to recognize when the signals they are getting are just friendly as opposed to 'ready for romance' cues.

Tip

Watch out for 'Please get away' signals, such as a woman who turns away from you or crosses her arms when you are about to kiss her.

The stages of sexual arousal

Flirting often does lead to sex, of course. And there is as much body language in the bedroom as in the boardroom. To understand intimate body language, it is worth looking at the work of two important researchers into sexual behaviour, William Masters and Virginia Johnson. They spent 20 years studying how our bodies respond before, during and after we make love.

In their lab, Masters and Johnson wired up volunteers and studied their pulse rate, skin response, eye dilation, erections, vaginal dilation, blood pressure and much else in sexual situations. Their results led them to develop a theory of the stages of sexual arousal.

The first two stages deal with the prelude to making love and are very clearly about body language. Stage 1 is arousal: the pulse races, breathing gets quicker, men begin to get an erection, women get tingly feelings, the pupils dilate. Animals have courtship rituals, but once they begin the sexual act it is usually quick. Human beings, however, enjoy pleasure and the anticipation of pleasure through foreplay. As foreplay intensifies, the tension builds and you wait, wait, wait for release.

Stage 2 is the plateau stage. Masters and Johnson named it this because foreplay builds to a pitch of excitement – a plateau, if you like. Most women and men have to spend time in this highly excited state before they can reach orgasm. As we start to make love, our bodies react in quite dramatic ways. Our breathing becomes quicker, our pupils dilate and the galvanic skin responses increase. There are also important changes in the genital area in both women and men.

When you are excited, it is not always easy to pay attention to your partner's body language. But it's wise to do so. Is he or she returning your kisses and your touching, or are you making every move first? Is there any sign that your partner is tense? Does he or she pull away?

It is hardly unusual to be anxious the first time you go to bed with someone. Very normal anxieties are:

- Is this happening too fast?
- Does he or she love me?

- Am I sexy enough?
- What does he or she expect of a sex partner?

The sensitive and smart thing is to be alert to any last-minute signs of stress or of displacement activity which suggests doubt.

Some of the most obvious signs of stress or doubt are shown by body alignment. In Figure 9.7, the couple are sitting side by side on the sofa but the man is clearly the keener, making all the 'come into my space' signals. He has an arm around her shoulder and his feet are turned in her direction, while she still has her ankles crossed tensely. In Figure 9.8 (overleaf), he has finally persuaded her to lean in against his shoulder. But her whole body is angled away from him and she's hunched her neck slightly so it's hard for him to kiss it.

Remember the acid test: you might be wrong. She may not see you as the man of her dreams but as just a nice, but not particularly fanciable, bloke. Men need to be especially sensitive and not to assume that they are going to 'score' in the next 60 seconds.

Figure 9.7   Body alignment 1

Figure 9.8   Body alignment 2

The robotic eye?

I want to end this chapter on a technological note. Some of us seek – and see – love in very strange places. A lecturer at the Society for Literature and Science in Pittsburgh, USA, in November 1997 reported that a woman found herself involuntarily *flattered* when a robot she was working on followed her with its camera eyes as she crossed the room. The machine seemed to love her – hurrah!

I now want to turn to a very different issue – lying. To get in the mood, just think how many words you can use for not telling the truth: lying, fibbing, making it all up, pretending, conning, deceiving, falsifying, fabricating, telling porkies ... Is it any accident that there are so many words for this particular human activity? I think not.

10

The body language of lying

The philosopher Friedrich Nietzsche said lying was a condition of life. Understanding body language can help us spot when people are lying – and we can learn to be better at this than lie detectors.

As you read this chapter, try to be honest about your motivation. In particular, face up to the following:

- Do you want to find out how to lie better?
- Or how to spot when people are lying to you?
- Or both?

In this chapter I look at:

- the psychology of lying;
- the six signs of lying.

The psychology of lying

We may not like to face up to this truth, but we are a lying species. Bella DePaulo (1994) of the University of Virginia and her colleagues asked 147 people (aged between 18 and 71) to keep diaries of all the falsehoods they told in one week. Most people lied once or twice a day. A fifth admitted that, if they spent more than ten minutes with someone else, they told a lie. During their week of (we hope but we doubt) honest self-observation, the diary-keepers deceived about 30 per cent of those they talked to. Extroverted, sociable people were slightly more likely to lie.

Relationships between teens and their parents are especially dishonest. 'College students lie to their mothers in one out of two conversations,' DePaulo reported.

We often justify lying on the grounds that it makes life easier for our loved ones: I know you love watching football on TV so I pretend I like it too. Couples who date lie to each other in about a third of their interactions. Sadly, but not surprisingly, we tell big lies to the people we are closest to. The person you love is probably the person you lie to most.

So, since most of us dislike being lied to, spotting the non-verbal cues that suggest someone is lying is important. Women, it seems, are naturally better at this and they are better at learning to improve their spot-the-lie skills. DePaulo asked pairs of same-sex friends to see if they could spot lies the other person told. Women's 'Am I being told a porkie?' detection skills improved slightly when her subjects were tested again six months later, but the men did not get better.

No one seems, however, to have dared do the killer study and look at whether men can tell when women are lying and women can tell when men are lying.

It is not just in personal situations that we need to spot whether someone is lying. In 1990 I made a film for Channel 4 called *The False Confessions File*. Someone leaked to me secret guidelines used by police forces to train detectives to spot the body language of lying. The tell-tale signs were said to be simple. Suspects who were lying tended to fidget, sweat and jiggle their knees (Figure 10.1).

I poked some fun at this in the film, as I imagined master criminals might have the sense not to fidget all the time.

Figure 10.1　A sign of lying: 'knee bobbling'

Emma Barrett, of *Psychology and Crime News*, has looked at recent research and discovered that much relies on looking at how Western students behave when deceiving in relatively low-stake situations. Research on whether law enforcement officers can detect deception usually involves them sitting in front of video clips of, you guessed it, Western students.'

It is different – and more encouraging – when the subjects are criminals rather than psychology students. Albert Vrij, Samantha Mann and their colleagues (2006) at Portsmouth University studied what happened when experienced police officers looked at video clips from real suspect interviews 'where ground truth was known' and the stakes were high. The officers wanted to get convictions and the suspects wanted to get away scot-free.

The police officers judged four sets of clips. In 72 per cent of cases they spotted lies. This is much better than the usual 50–60 per cent hit rate typically found in deception studies. Officers were equally good at detecting truth (70 per cent accuracy). Ironically, given how well they were doing, the officers tended to think they were not being that accurate and tended to be 'overly modest about, rather than overconfident in, their performance,' Emma Barrett noted. They made mistakes when they relied too much on too obvious cues, the kind I poked fun at in my film, including signs of nervousness and, yes, knee bobbling.

In 1991 Paul Ekman told the *New York Times* that one reason it is hard to spot lies is that 'the fear of being disbelieved looks the same as the fear of being caught lying'. An innocent person under stress who is desperate to be believed may well also fidget and even bobble their knees.

Psychologists have tried hard to come up with an infallible guide to whether you are being lied to. Burgoon, Knapp and Miller (1994) argue that there are six different non-verbal clues that someone is lying.

Six signs of lying

1 Cues that indicate you are anxious, like fidgeting or, as Joe Navarro (2003) observed, touching the back of your neck or your nose.

2   Cues that suggest you are being reticent or withdrawing from the situation, such as looking down.
3   Behaviours that are very different from the way you normally behave.
4   Behaviours that suggest you dislike what you are doing.
5   Cues showing underlying vagueness. A very clear one is when you hesitate for a long time before saying something or appear uncertain.
6   Incongruous responses or mixed messages.

Some personality factors also correlate with lying. People who are self-confident tend to lie better when they are under pressure, as do people who are more physically attractive.

The phrases people use may also give clues. James W. Pennebaker (2001), of Southern Methodist University in the USA, studied the words people choose when they lie. Liars tended to use fewer first-person words (like 'I' or 'my') and were less likely to use emotional words (such as 'hurt' or 'angry'), cognitive words (like 'understand' or 'realize') and so-called exclusive words (such as 'but' or 'without': words that distinguish what is and what is not).

So it is time to be honest with yourself about lying and body language.

Exercise 10.1: Self-observation – the lying quiz

1   I tell lies
    (a)   hardly ever;
    (b)   only when I have no alternative;
    (c)   quite often;
    (d)   very often.

2   When I tell a lie, I feel
    (a)   guilty;
    (b)   not too bothered.

3   If I think someone is lying to me, I watch carefully
    (a)   to see if they are looking straight at me;
    (b)   to see if there are any changes in their voice;
    (c)   to see if they start to fidget.

4   If someone says they don't believe me, I tend to
    (a)   react guiltily;

(b) tough it out by smiling at them;
(c) tell them not to be so silly.

5 I last told a lie
    (a) minutes ago;
    (b) last week;
    (c) so long ago I can't remember.

6 I tell lies
    (a) to spare people pain;
    (b) because I can get away with it;
    (c) because I don't want any one to really know what I think or feel;
    (d) because it makes me feel superior.

7 Which profession tells least lies?
    (a) journalist;
    (b) politician;
    (c) doctor.

8 I have to work myself up to tell a lie
    (a) never;
    (b) quite often;
    (c) always.

9 'Thou shalt not bear false witness'
    (a) was fine for the olden days of the Bible;
    (b) is not a commandment anyone takes seriously now;
    (c) is good advice.

10 If someone says, 'I never lie'
    (a) I admire them;
    (b) I require proof;
    (b) I know they're lying.

Answers
Work out your score by counting the number of Ts and Fs in your responses, according to the following:

Q1 (a) T; (b) X; (c) L; (d) F.
Q2 (a) T; (b) F.
Q3 no score.
Q4 (a) T; (b) X; (c) F.
Q5 (a) F; (b) T; (c) F.

Q6   (a) X; (b) F; (c) F; (d) F.

Q7   no score.

Q8   (a) F; (b) X; (c) T.

Q9   (a) F; (b) F; (c) T.

Q10   (a) T; (b) F; (c) F.

The more Ts you score, the more you think telling the truth is a good idea. The more Fs, the more of a liar you are – and proud of it. (Ignore X and L, which indicate lying under pressure and a muddled response.) Questions 3 and 7 do not really affect those issues but tell you something about your perception of liars.

Body language can help you spot lies but how does it help you lie effectively? You need to become very aware of what you do when you tell lies. The best advice I can give is to avoid exhibiting any of the six signs of lying on page 133 when you are lying.

11

Cross-cultural body language

We live in a multicultural society in an interdependent world. This means we need to understand the body language of different cultures, as misunderstanding can cause confusion and conflict.

When you are dealing with Chinese or Japanese or Saudi people, for example, you should remember they have a different sense of personal space (Figure 11.1). In northern Europe it is considered impolite to be closer than 1.33 metres to someone else unless you are intimate. In southern Europe, and especially in Arab countries, personal space is far smaller. If you stand too far away from someone, that seems rude.

But some aspects of body language are the same all over the world. Even in New Guinea people recognize Western expressions of anger, sadness, fear and joy, though in one study some of the allegedly primitive tribesmen were confused between surprise and fear expressions.

Figure 11.1 Personal space in different cultures

137

The way someone looks always conveys information about the self, especially about sex, age and social status. Certain cultures, however, may limit what information should be transmitted non-verbally. In Japan, for example, non-verbal communication is expected to carry information about status but not about feelings.

Michael Argyle, my old teacher, studied the way English, Italian and Japanese performed when they looked at emotional expressions on faces. English and Italian subjects could identify their own and each other's emotions but found it hard to read the Japanese, and even the Japanese themselves were not brilliant at identifying the emotional expressions of other Japanese people. The reality is not that the Japanese are always inscrutable, but that they are inscrutable in public and tend not to show what they feel when anyone else is looking. It used to be much the same in British public schools.

To confirm this, the ever ingenious Paul Ekman investigated whether there were differences between American and Japanese subjects while they watched horror films meant to provoke fear and disgust. When they thought they were alone, the Japanese showed revulsion and looked scared and upset, just like average Americans. But when the Japanese subjects watched the film with someone else present, they tended to smile to mask their feelings of disgust and fear (Ekman and Friesen, 1971).

If facial expressions mean much the same the world over, this is not true of expressions of the body. If you want to look at two cultures, imagine what happens when Sheikh Yamani from Cairo meets Mr Yamamoto from Tokyo.

Mr Yamamoto is used to Japanese conversation, which involves a great deal of ritual and prescribed answers. Also, as we have seen, it is not polite for Japanese people to show emotions in public – especially negative emotions. A poker face is considered ideal in public; in private a faint smile is acceptable. The Japanese also make less eye contact than the rest of us. Instead, they look at the neck. In particular they avoid looking at the faces of their superiors. They fidget if they have to gaze into an interviewer's eyes, 'reflecting the upsetting effects' of eye-to-eye contact (Bond and Komai 1976: 1276). Japanese society is loosening up and there is a big punk scene, but hierarchy still matters: Japanese men and women take great care to establish the correct relation-

Figure 11.2   The Japanese bow

ship by the right degree of bowing and the right tone of voice. They still bow when they meet someone (Figure 11.2), and the depth and duration of the appropriate bow depends on their relative status.

In the British House of Commons, no MP may call another MP a liar. The same inhibition is found everywhere in Japan. But sometimes Mr Yamamoto needs to say someone is lying, and when he does there is a gesture which is acceptable. He will lick his forefinger and stroke his eyebrow (Scollon and Wong-Scollon 1994).

Touching also varies between cultures. In public places in Japan there is very little bodily contact, not even handshakes. Contrast all this with the Arab countries, where there is more touching and less privacy than in the West. Like the Japanese, Arabs are also very sensitive to non-verbal behaviour but Arab men have few problems showing their feelings. They sometimes act in ways we in the West see as berserk, going so far as to tear at their clothing and scream in public.

I saw some of that in my childhood. My father was an Arab Jew who had been born in Palestine in 1908, when it was ruled by the Sultan in Istanbul. My father could be physically very demonstrative, hugging me as if our lives depended on it. But he could also yell and scream like a demented dervish. Once, when he had lost a lot of money on the stock market, he yelled so loudly that the neighbours knocked on our door. They wondered – in a polite British way – if someone was being murdered. The scene was especially surreal because my father had taken off his trousers and was shouting in his long-johns. My mother, who came from the Balkans and was educated in France, often called my father a barbarian because she found his displays of anger so bizarre. Incidentally, my father was not a camel trader but a lawyer with a PhD, but under stress, he reverted to childhood ways.

In conversation, two Arab men will look into one another's eyes more than would two Americans or two Englishmen (Argyle 1975). Males will touch one another on the arm or hand, particularly to emphasize a point or a joke. When they greet each other, men will often hold hands loosely (Figure 11.3) and may even kiss if they have not seen one another for some time. Some gestures also have particular meanings: for example, by bringing the tips of the upward-pointing thumb and fingers of one hand together to form a pyramid, and shaking the hand up and down from the wrist is a sign that a man thinks a woman is beautiful.

Figure 11.3 Male Arab body language

I was exposed to this florid body language when I was 16 and had to meet a distant cousin of my father's at the posh Dorchester Hotel. The man, who was a millionaire, insisted on holding my hand for ten minutes. I'd only met him once before, and I was mortified.

These very different styles of body language make it complicated for Arabs and Japanese to communicate easily. An Arab who tries to show respect by holding the gaze of a Japanese person will offend him, for instance. Sheikh Yamani will think it is acceptable to show how he feels, but Mr Yamamoto will think a man who emotes so much is either insane or impolite.

If you are going to do business abroad, it is wise to mug up on local customs in non-verbal communication. I have come across a number of gestures that I initially had no idea it was unwise to make.

Do not go on holiday to Greece and extend your arms horizontally, palms down, towards someone else. This is an insult which says, 'Go to hell twice.' Other palm-down gestures have specific cultural meanings, including the widespread *hand wag* for 'No!', the Saudi *hand slap* showing contempt, and the Italian *forearm thrust*, used as a sexual insult. Italians also touch their ears to suggest a man is effeminate.

In Portugal and Spain, if you tilt your head sideways and put your cheek in the palm of your hand you are saying that the person opposite is a weak-livered sissy. Again, avoid that one!

We also need to remember – and be alive to – the fact that the world is changing, sometimes for the better and in unexpected ways.

Shock horror! Greek lady touches me!

I sat in a small café in the centre of Athens. I had already downed one small brandy and wanted another. The elderly owner paid no attention to me even though I waved my arm up in the air, and I was getting annoyed because this utterly obvious signal was being ignored. So I got up, walked over and said, 'May I have another brandy, please?'

Figure 11.4   Touching to communicate

The grey-haired lady then did something that surprised me: she put her hand on my arm (Figure 11.4).

I was astonished. I felt as if she had made a truly indecent suggestion in front of the Greek pastries, but I had the sense to see it was not any kind of come-on. She was a respectable woman in her fifties running a respectable café. She wanted, I realized, to apologize for having neglected me. She didn't have the English and I didn't have the Greek – so she held my arm for five or ten seconds. I smiled at her and she smiled back – that simplest of human exchanges. Two minutes later, a very large brandy and a particularly gooey chocolate goodie were placed in front of me.

In the 1970s Greek women in their fifties tended to dress in grandma-black sacks from which they would never emerge. It would have been indecent for a respectable middle-aged Greek woman to touch a male stranger's flesh (I forgot to explain I was sleeveless).

The fact that the lady touched my bare arm suggests some taboos are dying in some cultures. Body language is a constant and is constantly changing.

12

The joy of understanding body language

I hope that by now my main message is clear. You need to learn how to analyse your own body language and how to observe that of your friends, lovers, brothers, sisters, parents and colleagues. This book should have given you the confidence to do it – and a good sense of what specific gestures mean.

It is not rocket science and it is fun. The main lessons remain:

- Pay attention not just to what people say but to every aspect of their behaviour.
- Use your eyes wisely – i.e. practise looking out of the corner of your eyes.
- Remember not to indulge in too much wishful thinking. The fact that someone smiles at you and takes your arm does not mean they necessarily want to sleep with you.
- Analyse your own body language 'habits'.
- Decide what aspects of your own body language may reveal things about yourself that you don't want to reveal.
- Learn to control the body language messages you give out.
- Use your answers to tests to analyse your own body language strengths and weaknesses. Then you can start to change and to deal with your weaknesses.
- Learn to laugh at your body language habits. Being able to laugh at yourself shows you have true self-confidence, the self-confidence that goes with being an MBL – a Maestro of Body Language.
- Enjoy the self-awareness – and awareness of others – that comes with this.

References

Argyle, M. *The Psychology of Interpersonal Behaviour*. Penguin, Harmondsworth, 1975

Bandler, R. and Grinder, J. *Frogs into Princes: Introduction to Neuro-Linguistic Programming*. Eden Grove Editions, London, 1990 (revised edition)

Beattie, G. *Visible Language*. Routledge, London, 2004

Blurton Jones N. *Ethological Studies of Child Behaviour*. Cambridge University Press, Cambridge, 1967

Bond, M. H. and Komai, H. 'Targets of gazing and eye contact during interviews: effects on Japanese nonverbal behavior'. *Journal of Personality and Social Psychology*, 34 (6): 1276–84 (1976)

Burgoon, J. K. 'Nonverbal signals'. In, M. L. Knapp and G. R. Miller (eds), *Handbook of Interpersonal Communication*. Sage, London, 2nd edn, 1994: 229–85.

Burt, D. M. and Perrett, D. I., 'Perceptual asymmetries in judgements of facial attractiveness, age, gender, speech and expression'. *Neuropsychologia*, 35: 685–93 (1997)

Caudillo, R., 'The perfect handshake'. *Nurse Week*, 4 August 2002.

Cohen, D. *Psychologists on Psychology*, Routledge, London, 1977

Cohen, D. 'The development of laughter'. Unpublished PhD thesis, University of London, 1985

Collett, P. *The Book of Tells*, Bantam, London, 2005

Darwin, C. *The Expression of the Emotions in Man and Animals*. John Murray, London, 1872

Davis, F. *Inside Intuition*. McGraw-Hill, New York, 1971.

DePaulo, B. M. 'Spotting lies: can humans learn to do better?'. *Current Directions in Psychological Science*, 3: 83–6 (1994)

DePaulo, B. M., Lindsay, J. J., Malone, B. E., Muhlenbruck, L., Charlton, K. and Cooper, H. 'Cues to deception'. *Psychological Bulletin*, 129: 74–118 (2003)

Duchenne, G. *Le Sourire*. Glyphe Editions, Paris, reprinted 2007

Ekman, P. and Friesen, W. V. 'Constants across cultures in the face'. *Journal of Personality and Social Psychology*, 17: 124–9 (1971)

Ekman, P. and Friesen, W. V. 'Felt, false and miserable smiles'. *Journal of Nonverbal Behavior*, 6: 238–52 (1982)

Ekman, P., O'Sullivan, M. and Frank, M. G. 'A few can catch a liar'. *Psychological Science*, 10: 263–6 (1999)

Elliot-Wright, S. *Overcoming Emotional Abuse*. Sheldon Press, London, 2007.

Eysenck, H. *Eysenck on Extraversion*, John Wiley, Chichester, 1973

Farroni, T., Csibra, G. and Johnson, M. H. 'Mechanisms of eye gaze perception during infancy'. *Journal of Cognitive Neuroscience*, 16: 1320–6 (2002)

Freud, S. *The Psychopathology of Everyday Life*. Hogarth Press, London, 1930

Gazzaniga, M. S. and Smylie, C. S. 'Hemispheric mechanisms controlling voluntary and spontaneous smiling'. *Journal of Cognitive Neuroscience*, 2: 239–45 (1990)

Goffman, E. *The Presentation of Self in Everyday Life*. Penguin, Harmondsworth, 1989

Goleman, D. 'Leadership that gets results'. *Harvard Business Review*. Harvard Business School Press, Cambridge, MA, 2002

Hall, Marny, quoted in Deborah A. Lott and Frank Veronsky, 'The new flirting game'. *Psychology Today*, Jan/Feb 1999

Hennenlotter, A. 'The neural mechanism of imagining facial affective expression'. *Brain Research*, 1145:128–37 (2007)

Higgins, P. *A Queer Reader*. Fourth Estate, London, 1993

Kendon, A. 'Gesture and understanding in social interaction'. *Research on Language and Social Interaction*, 27: 171–4 (1994)

LaFrance, M. <www.voanews.com>, 12 March 2000

Laing, R. D. *Knots*. Penguin, London, 1970

Lawick-Goodall, J. van, *In the Shadow of Man*. Dell, New York, 1974

Levi, P. *The Periodic Table*. Penguin, Harmondsworth, 2000

McCracken, G. *Big Hair*. Orion, London, 1997

Machiavelli, N. *The Prince*. Oxford University Press, Oxford, 2005

Masters,W. and Johnson, V. *Masters and Johnson on Sex and Human Loving*. Little Brown, New York

Mehrabian, A. *Non-Verbal Communication*. Walter de Gruyter, The Hague, 1972

Moore, M. 'Courtship signaling and adolescents: "Girls just wanna have fun"'. *Journal of Sex Research*, 32 (4): 319–28 (1995)

Morris, D. *The Naked Ape*. Jonathan Cape, London, 1967

Mueller, R. *Bullying Bosses: A Survivor's Guide*. Available via <www.bullyingbosses.com> 2005

Navarro, J. 'Universal principles of criminal behaviour: a tool for analyzing criminal intent'. *Research Forum FBI Law Enforcement Bulletin*, January 2003

Paradiso, S. *et al.* 'Frontal lobe syndrome reassessed'. *Journal of Neurology, Neurosurgery and Psychiatry*, 67: 664–7 (1999)

Pennebaker, J. W. 'Patterns of natural language use'. *Current Directions in Psychological Science*, 10: 90–4 (2001)

Pepys, S. *The Diary of Samuel Pepys*. HarperCollins, London, 1995

Perper, T. 'Flirting fascination'. *Psychology Today*, Jan/Feb 1999

Phillips, K., and Diaz, Z. 'Gender differences in body dysmorphic order'. *Journal of Nervous and Mental Disease*, 185: 570–7 (1997)

Piaget, J. *The Psychology of Intelligence*. Routledge, London, 1952

Preyer, W. *The Mind of the Child*. Houghton Mifflin, Boston, 1909

Schroeder, J. 'Consuming representation: a visual approach to consumer research'. In Barbara B. Stern (ed.) *Representing Consumers: Voices, Views and Visions*. Routledge, London, 1998: 193–230

Scollon, R., and Wong-Scollon, S. *Intercultural Communication*. Blackwell, Oxford, 1994

Tannen, D. *You Just Don't Understand*. Virago, London, 1992

Tinbergen, N., and Tinbergen, E. *Early Childhood Autism*. Taylor and Francis, London, 1972

Treleaven, P. C., Furnham, A., and Swami, V. 'Science of body metrics', *Psychology Magazine*, 19 (7): 416–19 (2006)

Valentine, C. W. *The Normal Child*. Penguin, Harmondsworth, 1970

Vrij, A. *Detecting Lies and Deceit: The Psychology of Lying and Its Implications for Professional Practice*. John Wiley, Chichester, 2000

Vrij, A., Mann, S., Robbins, E., and Robinson, M. 'Police officers' ability to detect deception in high stakes situations and in repeated lie detection tests'. *Journal of Applied Cognitive Psychology*, 20: 741–55 (2006)

Zajonc, R. 'Hot cognitions'. *Psychology News*, 1: 3 (October 1979)

Index

148 Index